Pursuing God's
Love

PARTICIPANT'S GUIDE

Also by Margaret Feinberg

The Organic God

The Sacred Echo:
Hearing God's Voice in Every Area of Your Life

Scouting the Divine:
My Search for God in Wine, Wool, and Wild Honey

Hungry for God:
Discovering God's Voice in the Ordinary and Everyday

Pursuing God's Beauty:
Stories from the Gospel of John DVD Bible Study

Margaret Feinberg

Pursuing God's
Love

PARTICIPANT'S GUIDE

Stories from the Book of
Genesis

ZONDERVAN®

ZONDERVAN.com/
AUTHORTRACKER
follow your favorite authors

We want to hear from you. Please send your comments about this book to us in care of zreview@zondervan.com. Thank you.

ZONDERVAN

Pursuing God's Love Participant's Guide
Copyright © 2011 by Margaret Feinberg

This title is also available as a Zondervan ebook. Visit www.zondervan.com/ebooks.

Requests for information should be addressed to:
Zondervan, *Grand Rapids, Michigan* 49530

ISBN 978-0-310-42823-7

Cover design: Kirk DouPounce
Cover photography: Getty Images
Interior design: Sherri Hoffman

Printed in the United States of America

11 12 13 14 15 16 /DCI/ 25 24 23 22 21 20 19 18 17 16 15 14 13 12 11 10 9 8 7 6 5 4 3 2 1

Contents

Special thanks to Evan Crass, Jennifer Rayner, and
Maegan Stout and their small groups for their valuable feedback
in the development of this study. Grateful for you!

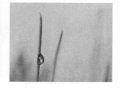

Pursuing God's Love

Stories matter. Your story matters. My story matters. But the greatest story we will ever encounter is the story of God's love for us.

Stories were passed down orally long before they were written down. Genesis was written so the Israelites would know God and his presence and involvement in people's lives since the beginning of the world. Through the Genesis story, the Israelites are reminded how they became God's people and discover God's tremendous love for them.

Why pursue God's love?

From the foundation of the world, God created us for love. Pursuing God's love isn't just about receiving God's love but recognizing that we were made for the purpose of loving God and loving others. We are meant to experience God's love and become expressions of God's love in our world.

According to tradition, Moses wrote the first five books of the Bible (also called the Torah), including Genesis, though some scholars believe that Genesis is a collection of writings from different authors.

The first book of the Bible probably isn't the oldest written book in the Bible. Many scholars believe the book of Job predates Genesis. Yet the title of this book is derived from the very first word of Scripture, *beresheet,* which means "beginning." Does the word refer to the beginning of time, space, creation, or our planet? While the answer is debated, we know that Genesis is primarily the story of God and an expression of the divine desire for a relationship with humankind. Genesis is a story we need to hear because it teaches us about the depth and breadth of God's love for us.

My hope and prayer is that through this study you'll be reminded of the depths of God's love and faithful commitment to you.

Blessings,

Margaret

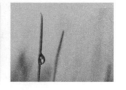

A Message for Leaders

The six sessions of *Pursuing God's Love* are designed to be accessible for people to grow in their knowledge of God and Scripture. Whether participants are still trying to figure out who God is or made the decision to follow Jesus decades ago, you'll find material that reaches them wherever they are in their spiritual journey.

Here are a few guidelines to help you and your group get the most out of this study.

Tailor the Study to Your Group

Groups are as diverse as the people in them. Some groups will want to watch one DVD session each week and complete the study in six weeks. Others may want to focus on the DVD one week and continue the discussion the next, creating a twelve-week study. Some groups will want to watch the DVD and then discuss as a large group; others will prefer to watch the DVD together and then break into smaller groups to discuss. Tailor the study to what best suits your group.

Select an Experiential Activity or Icebreaker Question in Advance

Each group session offers two options for getting started: an Experiential Activity or a selection of Icebreaker Questions. If your gathering is an hour or less, you may want to skip the activity or icebreaker question and dive right into the DVD so you have plenty of time for discussion. If your gathering is longer than an hour, select either the activity or one of the questions for your group.

Before the first meeting, read through all the experiential activities in the study. Select the ones you'd like to do and make a list of items you need to purchase, gather, or research.

Consider inviting a handful of participants to organize the experiential activity each week. This will encourage involvement and develop leadership skills of the participants.

Select Discussion Questions in Advance

Each session includes a variety of discussion questions. Some questions focus on encouraging people to open up about their lives and others focus more on wrestling with Scripture and the material presented on the DVD.

More questions are provided than time will allow for most groups — don't feel like you have to ask every question. Before you gather, highlight the questions you want to focus on during the session. Select the questions best suited to the interests and objectives of your group. You may even want to develop a few questions of your own.

As you lead the discussion, remember that silence can be a friend. You may ask a question and be greeted with silence. Allow the silence to rest for a moment and see who speaks up. If you have a participant who is particularly quiet and you're asking an open-ended question that anyone could answer, consider calling on that person by name. Gently ask, "What do you think, Josh?" Try to avoid questions that lead to "yes" and "no" answers, and stay focused on learning more about God and deepening relationships.

Throughout the study, you'll discover quotes, scholarly observations, and various insights. Invite discussion on the content of these boxes and see what develops.

Encourage Participants to Engage in Afterhours Personal Studies (If They Can)

Each session includes five Afterhours personal studies. The goal of Afterhours is to challenge participants to keep diving deeper into the book of Genesis. Encourage participants to engage in the personal studies, but remember that not everyone will be able to do so.

Remind participants that even if they aren't able to do Afterhours, they're still welcome to be part of the study. If they can only do one personal study each week, encourage them to complete Day Five, which specifically prepares participants for the next group session.

Stay Connected

Encourage participants to connect with Margaret on her website at *www.margaretfeinberg.com*, via Twitter @mafeinberg, or "like" her on Facebook. If you get a chance, take a photo of your group and submit it to be posted on the home page of her website. Email your photo to *info@margaretfeinberg.com* and include the name of your church or group.

God Rising

Genesis 1–3

> God loves us as we are, as he finds us, which is messy, muddy, and singing out of tune. Even when we've tried to be good, we have often only made matters worse, adding pride to our other failures. And the never-ending wonder at the heart of genuine Christian living is that God has come to meet us right there, in our confusion of pride and fear, of mess and muddle and downright rebellion and sin.[1]
>
> *–N. T. Wright*

Scripture is God's story. God is the central character, and God is the author of it all. Yet, as a loving God, we're invited into the divine story God has been writing since the beginning of time.

The opening chapters of Genesis are chock-full of stories that showcase the attributes of God. God is all-powerful, all-knowing, abounding in imagination, creativity, mystery, and wisdom. God is the source of life, strength, and goodness. God is immortal and transcendent. God has a plan and purpose. The first stories in Genesis remind us that even when we question, disobey, or doubt divine love, God continues pursuing us.

Getting Started: Select One

Experiential Activity: Imagining the Flavors of Eden

What you'll need:

- ◆ A variety of fresh fruits and vegetables
- ◆ Serving plates, forks, napkins

1. Visit a local supermarket that specializes in fresh produce. Buy a variety of fruits and vegetables. Be adventurous! Purchase some exotic fruits that you've never tried before.

2. Wash and prepare the fruits and vegetables prior to your gathering, or you may wish to leave everything whole and make cutting and peeling part of the group experience.

3. Discuss the following questions as you enjoy tasting your healthy snacks:

   - Which fruit is the most pleasing visually? Why?
   - Why do you think God created so many different types and flavors of fruits?
   - What emotions do you imagine God felt as creation unfolded?
   - After the man and woman were expelled from the garden, what are some of the things you think they missed most?

Icebreaker Question

If you're not doing the experiential activity, choose one *of the following questions to begin your discussion.*

- Imagine that you had the opportunity to stand alongside God on one of the days of creation. Which day of creation would you most like to experience and why?
- What kinds of activities help you appreciate the wonder of God's creation?
- What do you love about God the most?

Romans 8:39

One: God Rising

As you watch the DVD, use the following outline to take notes on anything that stands out to you.

When I face times like those in life, the only thing I know to do is not give up.

In some ways, Genesis is the greatest love story ever told because it reminds us that God's love for humankind cannot be thwarted.

I apologized profusely, but hung up the phone with that sense of, "What have I done?"

As a holy and divine artist, God paints our world beautiful with the most loving attention to detail.

Whenever we focus on God's prohibitions rather than provisions, we can't help but doubt the goodness and generosity of God. We can't help but question God's love.

While the story in the garden is often referred to as "the fall of humankind," I can't help but think we need to rename it "God's rising."

††† Group Discussion Questions

(30–45 MINUTES)

1. What caught your attention or stood out most to you on the DVD?

Going Nowhere

2. The spiritual life is marked by seasons of growing and making great progress as well as those seasons when it doesn't feel like any progress is being made. Use the sentence starters to briefly describe both experiences.

   I know I'm growing spiritually when ...

   I know I'm stalled spiritually when ...

3. How do you typically respond when you mess up?

   Are you able to accept forgiveness (from God and others) and move on, or are you more likely to beat yourself up with regret and second-guessing?

What helps you to move beyond your mistakes?

Notable

Many scholars believe that Genesis was written for a people living in exile and meant to refute the false theological claims of the Babylonians. That it was written for a people who were discouraged and felt defeated. The first chapter of Genesis is a powerful declaration that God is the Lord of all.

The Story of God

4. When you read the Bible, do you tend to view what you're reading as a historical document, a scientific document, a theological document, a literary document, or some other way? Explain.

5. How does the way you tend to view the Bible affect the way you learn about God and grow spiritually?

6. Read Genesis 3:1–7. It's easy to recognize that Adam and the woman fell for the serpent's lie that God isn't good or doesn't really love them, but what relationships or situations tend to challenge *your* belief in God's goodness or love for you?

7. Deep down inside, do you really believe God loves you? Explain.

God Rising

8. Overall, would you say you tend to focus more on God's prohibitions or God's provisions in your life? Mark your response on the continuum below. Briefly share the reason for your response.

I AM ALWAYS AWARE OF
GOD'S PROHIBITIONS.

I AM ALWAYS AWARE OF
GOD'S PROVISIONS.

9. Do you tend to focus more on your failings or on the redemptive healing and restoration God offers you? Mark your response on the continuum below. Briefly share the reason for your response.

I ALWAYS FOCUS MORE
ON MY FAILINGS.

I ALWAYS FOCUS MORE ON THE
REDEMPTIVE HEALING AND
RESTORATION GOD OFFERS ME.

Why is it important to focus on God's rising more than our failings?

When have you most recently experienced God rising in your own life?

Quotable

"The Bible is the story of the creation of the universe — brilliant, glistening, new, and green — and of our own creation in the image of God. It is the story of our falling away from God and of God's repeated attempts to bring us back."[2]

–H. Stephen Shoemaker

10. How are you actively and intentionally pursuing God's love in your life and your relationships right now?

At times, we need to shift our focus from our mistakes to God's rising—the ability of God to heal, redeem, and make a way for us. When we do, we find God's love pouring more readily to us and through us.

 ## Close in Prayer

Ask God to:

- Give you the spiritual eyes to see the wonders of creation.
- Provide a new appreciation for God's rising in your life.
- Open up new opportunities to both receive and extend God's love.

Jumpstart

To get an insider's look at the Pursuing God series, bonus features, and freebies, as well as join the online discussion, visit *www.pursuinggodbiblestudy.com*.

To prepare for the next group session, read Genesis 4 and tackle the After-hours personal studies.

> **Bonus Activity**
>
> Take a quick photo! Before you close, take a picture of your group and email it to *info@margaretfeinberg.com*. Your group could be featured on the home page of *www.margaretfeinberg.com*.

* Judy - Mexico
* Praise for Kimberly's dad
* travels for Katie's husband
* Mary B - healing
* our teenagers
* Katie's brother Micha
* Wendy

Afterhours Personal Studies

Dive deeper into the book of Genesis by engaging in these five personal studies. If you only have time for one, choose Day Five, which will prepare you specifically for the next session.

DAY ONE: The Breathtaking Account of Creation

Genesis 1:1–2:3

The opening chapter of Genesis provides a breathtaking account of the story of creation. This is the story of God bringing order to our world. The creation story is a powerful reminder that everything God creates has a purpose.

Each day of the creation story follows a pattern, which often includes *announcing, commanding, separating, reporting, naming, evaluating,* and *timing.* However, some days of creation provide exceptions to the pattern. For example, day two in the creation story is the only day in which God doesn't say, "It is good" (Genesis 1:6–8). Scholars differ on the explanation. Some suggest that day two isn't declared good because there is a separation between the heavens, or firmament, and the water below. They argue that any separation from heaven isn't good. Whatever the reason, it's worth paying attention to the exceptions found in the pattern used to describe creation.

1. Read Genesis 1. On day three, God says "It is good" twice. What do you think was good about creating the tree of life and the tree of knowledge of good and evil (Genesis 2:16–17)?

2. On which day of creation does God declare what he creates "very good" (Genesis 1:31)?

Why do you think this day receives a special declaration?

3. Which day of creation is mentioned three times, indicating its significance (Genesis 2:2–3)?

   What is the first thing God creates that he sets apart as holy (Genesis 2:3)?

   In what ways have you experienced the Sabbath as a holy day in your own life?

4. What is the only day of creation that does not include, "There was evening, there was morning" (Genesis 2:2–3)?

   Why do you think this phrase is omitted?

5. What obstacles in your life prevent you from entering God's rest?

In ancient culture, the sun, moon, and stars were often worshipped as gods. It is important to make a distinction between the objects that produce light and God as the source of light. Note the sequence of creation: God creates light itself on day one, but it isn't until day four that he hangs the sun, moon, and stars in the sky.

The creation story is laced with details that highlight the wonders of God. It teaches us that God exists within himself, triumphs over chaos, and is intimately involved with creation. While other gods threaten death and loss, our God is full of blessing. God's creation literally teams with life.

6. In which areas of your life do you need to experience God triumphing over chaos?

How do you hope to experience God's blessing in these areas?

Spend some time thanking God for any fresh insights or discoveries you made as you dove into the first chapter of Genesis. Ask God to give you the desire and time to dive deeper into the Scriptures over the upcoming week. Ask the Holy Spirit to illuminate Genesis as you read and study.

DAY TWO: A Second Account of Creation

Genesis 1–2

If the first chapter of Genesis provides a bird's eye view of the story of creation, then the second chapter provides a street-level view as it continues the story of creation, adding rich details to the creation of the garden and humankind.

An interesting shift in perspective takes place from Genesis 1 to Genesis 2. The first chapter of Genesis tells the creation story from God's perspective; the second chapter of Genesis tells the story from a human perspective. While Genesis 1:1 notes that in the beginning God created "the heavens and the earth," Genesis 2 reverses the order: "the earth and the heavens" (2:4).

1. Read Genesis 1–2. As you read, make a list of four to six differences you notice in the way the two chapters tell the creation story.

2. How does the Genesis 2 account of creation expand your understanding of God and the purpose of humankind? (*Hint:* See Genesis 2:15–17.)

> **Notable**
>
> Men and women have the same number of ribs anatomically. But since Adam and Eve were the first people, it's always fair to wonder, did they have bellybuttons?

3. How should knowing that you're made in "the image of God" (see Genesis 1:26–27; 2:22–25) affect the way you interact and view the following:

Yourself...

Others...

God...

4. Some scholars note a correlation between the words and phrases used in the story of creation and the words and phrases used in the Exodus story of the tabernacle. The tabernacle was a portable sanctuary, God's temporary dwelling place among his people before they were able to build a permanent temple. Scholars suggest that the temple is a smaller portrait of what God created in the beginning of Genesis. Look up the following passages. What common words and phrases do they share?

Passages	Shared words and phrases
Genesis 1:31 and Exodus 39:43	
Genesis 2:1 and Exodus 39:32	
Genesis 2:2 and Exodus 40:33	
Genesis 2:3 and Exodus 39:43	

When God instructs the Israelites to build the tabernacle, God is renewing the vision of the garden of Eden, the vision of God dwelling with humanity.

5. When are you most aware of God's desire to be with you? How do you respond when you sense the Spirit's tugging in your life?

God places Adam in the garden of Eden, which can be translated "pleasure" or "delight," and instructs him to enjoy the lush fruits and vegetables of the land, except for one: the fruit of the tree of knowledge of good and evil. Though the tree of life is mentioned first in the text, all the attention falls on the second tree — suggesting that mankind's desire for power is stronger than his hunger for life.

6. When do you feel most tempted by the desire for power?

Spend some time thanking God for the wonders and beauty of creation. Praise God for the care and love with which humankind was made. Ask God to increase your own desire for an intimate relationship with God as well as the abundant life God wants to give you.

DAY THREE: Facing Temptation

Genesis 3:1–7

The third chapter of Genesis paints a beautiful portrait of God's love for us by demonstrating divine grace and provision for our lives. We meet God's adversary who takes the form of a serpent. The Genesis text never says that Satan is the actual snake in the garden, but in the Old Testament and the New, snakes are sometimes used to describe evil people or nations. However, in the last book of the Bible, Satan is described as a snake (Revelation 12:9, 13–15). Satan could have chosen to take the form of any animal, but chooses a wise, crafty reptile.

1. Read Genesis 3:1–3 and compare it to Genesis 2:16–17. How does the serpent distort God's instructions?

> **Notable**
>
> The Hebrew word for "knowing" is *yodea*, which can also be translated as a respectful reference to a divine being. The temptation of the serpent in Genesis 3:5 can be interpreted as a promise to become "divine beings, knowers of good and evil."

2. Read Genesis 3:4–5. The serpent is a smooth talker. In just a few sentences, he convinces the woman to doubt God's goodness and embrace disobedience. What do you think was most appealing to the woman about the serpent's argument in this passage?

Which aspect of the temptation would be the hardest for you to resist?

The serpent approaches the woman with a mixture of truth and falsehood. The woman turns to the tree, rather than God, to make her final decision. She finds the fruit is aesthetically pleasing and tasty. She shares the news with her husband. The Scripture doesn't detail their conversation, and so we are left to wonder: Did Adam protest? Did the woman disclose which fruit the tree was plucked from? Were the serpent's arguments enough to convince Adam? Did the woman add any arguments to persuade Adam to eat the fruit?

3. Read Genesis 3:6–7. In the space below, imagine and record the dialogue between the woman and Adam in which she convinces him to eat the fruit. For example:

THE WOMAN: *"Honey, you'll never guess what I discovered in the garden today! The fruit on this one tree is sweeter and more delicious than anything we've eaten so far."*

ADAM: *"You know that I love fruit—which tree did you get it from?"*

THE WOMAN:

ADAM:

THE WOMAN:

ADAM:

THE WOMAN:

ADAM:

Which argument do you imagine was most effective in convincing Adam to eat the fruit?

> **Notable**
>
> Some scholars believe the tree of life extended life rather than granted immortality. Being removed from the garden prevented access to the tree. This interpretation explains why God never forbid Adam and Eve not to eat the fruit of the tree of life.

Though we don't know the details of the conversation between Adam and the woman, both ate the fruit. The consequences of their actions were just as God had warned—death entered the world. Their eyes were opened as they were given the knowledge of good and evil. In an instant, they experience something they've never encountered before: shame. What is shame? The painful feeling of embarrassment, humiliation, or distress resulting from the awareness of wrong, foolish, or ill-considered behavior.

4. What types of situations or encounters have caused you to feel shame?

5. The Bible is rich with promises about how God wants to remove our shame. Read Psalm 119:39, Romans 8:1–2, Romans 10:11, and John 8:1–11. How do these promises encourage you?

Spend some time asking God to reveal any interactions or incidents from the past for which you still feel shame. Ask God to remove any shame and saturate you with forgiveness, grace, and hope.

DAY FOUR: The Story of God

Genesis 3:8–24

A crafty serpent convinces the woman of the ultimate lie, namely, that God is not good. She and Adam eat the fruit. Sin enters our world. Stripped of their innocence, the couple attempts to cover themselves. They reach for the bright green fig leaves—which are known to grow up to a foot in length—to create a covering. The couple is alienated from each other and God as they hide among the vegetation.

While the story of the garden is often called "the fall," a better name might be "God's rising." Remember that this is God's story: "In the beginning ... God." While Genesis 3 highlights our sinful nature and a tragic decision on the part of humankind, the hero of the story is still God. A glimpse of God's plan for redemption emerges in the promise that one of the woman's offspring will crush the head of the serpent.

1. Despite their sin, God does not abandon Adam, the woman, or the garden. Read Genesis 3:8–13. What four questions does God ask?

God's four questions
1.
2.
3.
4.

If God already knows the answer to these questions, why do you think God chose to ask them anyway?

What does the interaction among God, Adam, and the woman reveal about God's love and his desire for a relationship with us?

Quotable

"The most lamentable result of sin to an Israelite is not that it makes people bad but that it makes God distant."[4]
– John H. Walton

2. Read Genesis 3:14–19. What does God curse in this passage? (*Hint:* See vv. 14, 17.)

3. Instead of cursing Adam or the woman, God makes several promises to them. List the promises God makes to the man and woman in the space below:

After God judges the serpent, the woman, and Adam, a subtle but significant shift takes place in the text. For the first time, the woman is given a personal name! She is called Eve, the mother of all the living. The name Eve is derived from the Hebrew word *chavah*, meaning "to breathe." This is the first sign of hope after the fall. God's redemptive work has begun. Eve will bear children. Many generations later one of her offspring will defeat evil forever.

A second sign of hope appears in God's provision for Adam and Eve. God takes on the role of fashion designer and creates clothing for them from animal skins. The scene foreshadows the central biblical truth that sin requires a sacrifice, which appears later in Scripture.

4. The third sign of hope is found in God's removal of Adam and Eve from the garden. Read Genesis 3:22–24. Why was driving the couple from the garden a sign of God's love and protection?

5. What are some unexpected ways in which you've experienced God's love and protection?

How do you tend to respond to difficult situations in life before you recognize God's love and protection in those things?

6. How might the difficult things in your life right now actually be a sign of God's love and protection?

Adam and Eve are removed from the garden forever. The great loss is not the garden but God. Throughout the rest of the Old Testament, we never read about people wanting to return to the comforts of Eden; instead they long for God's presence. As Genesis continues to unfold, we keep seeing God rising—divine love and redemption appearing in the most unexpected circumstances and situations.

Spend some time reflecting on any areas of your life where you need to experience God rising. Ask God to increase your awareness of divine love.

DAY FIVE: Cain's Legacy

Genesis 4

The story of Cain and Abel is a story of heartbreak—two brothers whose differences cause one to murder the other. In the wake of the fratricide, the story makes it clear that the descendants of Cain will continue to compound their sins until hope appears and God's people begin to love and obey him.

1. Read Genesis 4:1–16. Reflecting on Genesis 4:1–5, why do you think Cain's gift wasn't highly regarded by God?

2. Though Scripture does not specifically tell us, what do you imagine happened between Cain and Abel in the field on the day Cain murdered his brother?

Not only does the story of Cain teach us about the importance of love, forgiveness, and obedience, it also gives us an insight into temptations we face. God tells Cain, "If you do what is right, will you not be accepted? But if you do not do what is right, sin is crouching at your door; it desires to have you, but you must rule over it" (Genesis 4:7).

3. Read the passages listed in the following chart. In the second column, note the wisdom each passage offers about handling anger. Then rate how difficult it is for you to apply this particular truth when you are angry. Use a scale of 1 to 10, with 10 being the most difficult.

Scripture	Wisdom about how to handle anger	Level of difficulty (1 to 10)
Proverbs 15:1	Ex.: Responding with gentleness can diffuse anger.	Ex.: 7
Proverbs 20:2		
Proverbs 21:14		
Proverbs 22:24		
Proverbs 29:11		
Ecclesiastes 7:9		
Matthew 5:21 – 24		
Ephesians 4:26 – 27		
James 1:20		

4. Reflecting on the Scriptures from the chart in question 3, list four to six ways Cain could have handled the situation differently.

Place a checkmark next to the passage that is most compelling for you. How might it help you to develop a healthier response to anger?

Whenever you encounter genealogies in Scripture, it's important to remember that they don't always include every single person who is born. They're more like a highlight reel. Biblical genealogies also serve more than one purpose. For example, they may trace lineage back to a common ancestor, establish continuity between biblical stories, demonstrate the legitimacy of a person for a particular office, or reveal God's redemptive work and favor in a person's life.

5. Read Genesis 4:17–26. What is the significance of the birth of Enosh?

What does it look like in your own life to call on the name of the Lord?

Spend some time in prayer asking God to reveal any areas of anger or unforgiveness in your life. Acknowledge what you've done or left undone. Ask God to forgive and heal you.

Call on the Name of the Lord

Genesis 4–11

God has made it a rule for Himself that He won't alter people's character by force. He can and will alter them — but only if the people will let him.... He would rather have a world of free beings, with all its risks than a world of people who did right like machines because they couldn't do anything else. The more we succeed in imagining what a world of perfect automatic beings would be like, the more, I think, we shall see His wisdom.[5]

—C. S. Lewis

In love, God gives us a choice. We are not forced to love God, but given a profound and life-shaping opportunity to love. At times we might be tempted to think that our lives would be easier or better if we were compelled to love God, but true love requires making a choice.

Will we love God? Or will we choose to love lesser gods? Will we choose to pursue God? Or will we choose to pursue someone or something else? God pursues us in love and we are given the opportunity to pursue God and divine love every day. When faced with this opportunity, the question becomes, what will we choose?

Getting Started: Select One

Experiential Activity: Discovering the Saint John's Bible

What you'll need:

- ◆ Information and images of the Saint John's Bible
- ◆ A laptop and video projector to display the images

1. Learn about the Saint John's Bible by visiting *www.saintjohnsbible.org.* Check the schedule to find out if the Saint John's Bible is on display in a city near you.
2. You'll find a brief video about the making of the Saint John's Bible by searching for "In the Beginning" and "St. John's Bible" on YouTube. Consider sharing the video with the group.
3. Talk about what you discover with the group.
4. Consider showing some of the images of the Saint John's Bible to participants and discuss the meaning of the symbols found in the illustrations.*

- • What inspires you about the Saint John's Bible project?
- • How do the illuminations help bring the Scriptures alive?
- • Which of the images shown is your favorite? Why?

---

*Be sure to note if there are any restrictions on duplicating the image or if it is necessary to secure permission to reproduce the image.

Icebreaker Question

If you're not doing the experiential activity, choose one *of the following questions to begin your discussion.*

- • Have you ever owned or encountered a Bible that was particularly meaningful to you? Describe what made it special to you.
- • Anger can reveal itself in a variety of ways, including facial expressions, body posture, and tone of voice. When Cain becomes angry his countenance falls. How can people tell if you're angry?
- • What are some of the biggest challenges that technology is creating in your life? In your relationships?

[handwritten: What does it look like to:]

[handwritten: in my world.] **(15 MINUTES)**

As you watch the DVD, use the following outline to take notes on anything that stands out to you.

Donald Jackson wanted to create a Bible that captured the beauty and tradition of centuries of liturgy and carry it into the future.

[handwritten: St. John's bible —]

While advancements in technology enhance our ability to absorb and share information and make our lives more convenient, they also create new challenges.

God doesn't ask questions to learn something new, but so we can learn something new about ourselves.

The man who refused to be his brother's keeper now has no one to keep him. The man who murdered now fears being murdered.

Technology is increasing and morality is decreasing.

We live in an age of great technological advancements, but maybe that's all the more reason to pursue God, to call on God.

Group Discussion Questions

1. Consider what you learned from God's love and pursuit of humanity through the Afterhours personal studies or on the DVD. What caught your attention or stood out most to you?

2. When have you been confronted with something inappropriate and unexpected because of technology?

   How did you respond to the situation?

God Pursues Abel

3. Read Genesis 4:1–8. What connection exists between the way Cain saw God and the way he treated Abel?

   Why is it important to have a healthy, accurate view of God?

4. When has a distorted view of God affected the way you see and treat others?

5. Read Genesis 4:9–16. What encouragement do you find in God's protection of Cain in the midst of his punishment (vv. 13–15)?

What does God's protection reveal about divine love and grace?

An Ancient Genealogy with Modern Implications

6. Participants can take turns reading the following passages aloud: Genesis 4:17–26; Matthew 18:21–22; Luke 17:3–4. Reflecting on the song of vengeance by Lamech (Genesis 4:23–24) and the Gospel passages, how do you think Jesus would respond to Lamech's song?

7. What types of situations are most difficult for you to choose to forgive?

Why is forgiveness important to you?

Calling on the Name of the Lord

8. What does it specifically look like for you to call on the name of the Lord while engaged in the following activities? (for example: *I prayerfully consider how much time to spend on social media.*)

Using social media such as Facebook or Twitter ...

Using your mobile phone ...

Shopping online ...

Surfing the Internet ...

Other ...

9. Apart from the use of technology, how do you call on the name of the Lord in daily life?

10. What prevents you from calling on the name of the Lord more often?

The story of Cain and Abel as well as the genealogy tucked into Genesis 4 are powerful reminders that though sin abounds, we can choose to be people who call on the name of the Lord. We do not have to allow sin to get the best of us—we can call on God and be the people who pursue God's love.

Close in Prayer

Ask God to:

- Bring to mind any areas of unforgiveness where you need to be forgiven.
- Give you wisdom and grace as you use technology.
- Prompt you to call on the name of the Lord more often.

Jumpstart

To get an insider's look at the Pursuing God series, bonus features, and freebies, as well as join the online discussion, visit *www.pursuinggodbiblestudy.com*.

To prepare for the next group session, read Genesis 12–23 and tackle the Afterhours personal studies.

* Gloria - Kim McGraw's mother
* Kimberly — dad aneurism/praise
Anna + Emily Robinson
Georgia community
* Mary Benson
* youth camp
* Wendy - depression

Afterhours Personal Studies

Dive deeper into the book of Genesis by engaging in these five personal studies. If you only have time for one, choose Day Five, which will prepare you specifically for the next session.

DAY ONE: Walking with God among the Generations

Genesis 5

Genealogies in the Bible often follow a pattern. When this happens in a genealogy, it's important to pay attention to any deviations from the pattern.

1. Read Genesis 5 and note how the narrative uses the basic genealogy pattern: naming a man who lives so many years, has children, and then dies. Use the chart to document the deviations from this basic genealogy pattern and why you think each deviation might be significant.

Scripture	Deviation	Significance
Genesis 5:3	Seth	
Genesis 5:24	Enoch	walked w/God – didn't die?
Genesis 5:29	Noah	brought the people comfort
Others?		physical walk vs. spiritual walk

2. What are some specific times in your life when you've experienced that kind of close and intimate relationship with God that Enoch experienced?

3. What does it look like to walk with God in your own life?

like walking w/a friend
physical vs spiritual

> **Notable**
>
> Enoch's name means "dedicated, vowed, or trained." Enoch is listed seventh, a position often given special attention in biblical genealogies.

4. What recent opportunities has God given you to be a source of comfort—like Noah (Genesis 5:29)—for others?

Enoch walks with God and doesn't die in the same way the others do. Enoch gives us the hope that if we walk with God, we too can get a reprieve from death. And Noah, a man whose name means "comfort," gives us the hope that we too can have a reprieve from living under a curse. This genealogy suggests that though we live in a fallen world and all of us will eventually die, we can find a reprieve if we walk with God just as Enoch and Noah did.

Spend some time in prayer asking the Lord to increase your desire for a more intimate and close relationship with God. Ask for opportunities to be a source of comfort to others. Keep your eyes open for the ways God answers that prayer over the upcoming week.

At the end of the Genesis 5 genealogy, we meet a new character, Noah, and enter into a new chapter in the story of God's redeeming work in the world. Sin still abounds on the earth, but God raises up a new generation who will call on the name of the Lord and walk in righteousness.

Before Noah's story begins, there is a brief "aside" in Genesis 6:1–4 about the Nephilim. Theories abound about this mysterious group, whose only other mention in Scripture is found in Numbers 13:32–33. The Hebrew word *nephilim* can be translated "fallen ones." Some believe they were supernatural beings from God's heavenly court, which would make the Nephilim fallen angels. Others believe they are descendants of Seth who are marked by their rebellion. In any case, their association in the Bible is not a positive one.

1. Read Genesis 6:1–22. What parallels do you see between this description of the corruption of humanity (Genesis 6:1–8) and that which appeared in Genesis 4:16–26 (also discussed in the DVD)?

2. Noah is described as a righteous man. How do Noah and his family compare with the corrupt people around them? (*Hint:* See Genesis 6:5, 8–9, 11–12.)

When have you found yourself standing in stark contrast to those around you because of your righteous choices?

How did you handle the situation?

3. Noah was surrounded by unrighteous people but chose to live righteously. When it comes to the unrighteous people in your life right now, would you say you are the influencer or the one being influenced?

4. Reflecting on Noah's story, in which relationships of your life do you need to invest more time and energy in order to be a godly influence? What personal relationships do you need to reevaluate because you're being negatively influenced by them?

Throughout the Noah narrative, God is not angered as much as grieved. Creation opposes divine purposes. Evil reigns in people's hearts. The pain experienced by Eve as described in Genesis 3:16 is now felt by God. 'Atsab, the Hebrew word used for Eve's "pain" in Genesis 3:16, is the same word translated as "grieve" (NASB) to describe God's anguish in Genesis 6:6. God is not an angry tyrant but a loving creator who grieves over what has become of creation.

5. In the first session, we learned that God has power over chaos. In the story of Noah, God uses a recognized force of chaos—raging waters—to overcome the human chaos of violence. What does God's care for Noah, his family, and all the living creatures reveal about God's love for creation and humanity?

In Genesis 6:18, the word "covenant" (berit) appears for the first time. God doesn't just establish a covenant; he calls it "my covenant." God takes ownership of the covenant. God promises to preserve Noah but, as part of the covenant, Noah must follow God's specific instructions and build an ark. The building of the ark is not only outrageously expensive but takes years to complete. This is an epic moment — not just for Noah and his family but for all of us. If Noah chooses to disobey, sleep in, or wait for plan B, God's divine purpose to bring salvation through the future generations will be derailed. Fortunately, Noah chooses to obey.

Consider the people you spend the most time with each day. Ask God for the strength and grace to be a reflection of God's righteousness in their lives. Look for opportunities to serve, practice generosity, and demonstrate God's love in tangible ways.

DAY THREE: **All Aboard the Ark**

Genesis 7–9

Building the ark was a monumental challenge, but imagine stepping aboard the ark with hundreds (if not thousands) of noisy, stinky animals. The gathering of the animals for the ark raises all of kinds of questions. Instead of addressing these concerns, the story focuses on God's intimate involvement and Noah's faithful obedience.

1. Read Genesis 7–8. (You may want to skim 6:14–22 first.) Reflect for a moment on the enormity of this project as well as some of the concerns, conflicts, and humorous situations that would emerge along the way. What questions does the story of the ark, the animals, and Noah's family raise? (for example: *What did Noah do when one animal tried to eat another?*)

2. Noah obeys God in the monumental project of building and filling the ark. What does this reveal about how he probably responded to God in smaller, day-to-day things?

Is it easier for you to trust God with a monumental project or smaller, day-to-day activities? Why?

After Noah, his family, and all the animals board the ark, God closes the door behind them. Imagine Noah's wife turning to confirm the door closed on its own after hearing it slam, and feeling goose bumps run and up down her spine. After months of preparation, building, and waiting, the moment arrives and God is still with them. The door-closing demonstrates the divine presence and protection as they embark into the unknown.

Genesis 8 begins with the words, "God remembered Noah." This remembering isn't just a fleeting thought that eight people are seasick inside a wooden contraption being tossed to and fro in the greatest flood the world has ever seen. The Hebrew word for remember, *zkr*, signifies God acting on a commitment because of a covenant relationship. God alone controls the flood and has not forgotten the promise to Noah.

As the waters subside, Noah releases two birds from the ark to find out whether or not it's safe to leave the vessel. The first is a raven, a bird eventually considered unclean according to the law of Moses (Deuteronomy 14:14). The second is a dove, a bird eventually considered clean according to the law of Moses and acceptable for the poor to offer as a sacrifice (Leviticus 5:7). When the dove is released and fails to return, Noah knows the land is dry. Noah's first act on dry land is to build an altar and worship. God promises to never again destroy every living thing with floodwaters and marks the covenant with a rainbow.

While the word "rainbow" is used to describe the sign of God's covenant in Genesis 9:13, the actual word in Hebrew is "bow," signifying a hunting instrument or battle weapon. This highlights a bit of irony since one of the reasons God destroyed humanity was because of their violence (Genesis 6:13). God turned a sign of hostility into a symbol of reconciliation and peace by symbolically hanging a divine bow in the sky.

3. Read Genesis 9:1 – 18. Then look up the Scriptures passages in the following chart and note the parallels between Adam and Noah.

Scriptures	Parallels between Adam and Noah
Genesis 3:8 and Genesis 6:9	Ex.: Both men walk with God.
Genesis 2:19 and Genesis 7:15	
Genesis 1:28 – 30 and Genesis 9:1 – 7	
Genesis 3:17 – 19 and Genesis 9:20	
Genesis 3:6 and Genesis 9:21	
Genesis 3:7 and Genesis 9:21	

What do the parallels reveal about God's faithfulness and love of humanity?

Though we aren't given the exact timing, Genesis 9:18 marks a shift in the story of Noah. Through Noah's sons—Shem, Ham, and Japheth—the earth is repopulated. Noah follows in the footsteps of Adam and cultivates the land. He becomes a vintner, growing grapes. After processing the harvest, Noah over-imbibes and becomes drunk. The Scripture says he then uncovers himself in his tent.

Just a few chapters earlier, Adam and Eve were running through the garden without clothes. After the fall, people are increasingly aware of their nakedness. Ham sees his father and tells his brothers, Shem and Japheth, who take a garment, walk backward, and cover their father without seeing him naked. Scholars debate why Ham's actions are considered so despicable. Some argue that Ham saw Noah and his wife being intimate and told the details to his brothers. Others suggest that something sexual happened between Ham and his father. Others suggest that something sexual happened between Ham and his mother.

The text is blank on this detail. All we know is that Ham did not preserve the dignity of his father as his brothers did. When Noah awakes, he curses Canaan, Ham's son. In other words, Ham's entire family line is affected. A man God used to bring comfort and to lift the curse of working the soil ends up cursing his own family line.

4. Read Genesis 9:19 – 29. What surprises you most about the ending of Noah's life story?

5. What warnings from the end of Noah's life story are most applicable in your own spiritual walk right now?

6. What aspects of Noah's character — obedience, hard work, faith, courage, hope, resilience, and patience — do you feel most in need of? Why?

Quotable

"Noah was a brave man to sail in a wooden boat with two termites."
– Unknown

Spend some time reflecting on Noah's story. Ask God to develop the character traits that you most appreciate about Noah in your own life.

DAY FOUR: Constructing a Tower to Heaven

Genesis 10–11

Genesis 10 records a genealogy of the sons of Noah. This genealogy reminds us that even in the darkest of times, God still has a redemptive plan. Though the world dies in the flood, God mercifully saves one family. Through their line, humanity is recreated.

1. Read Genesis 10. Reflecting on what you've learned so far about gene-alogies from the DVD as well as the personal studies, what catches your attention in this genealogy?

While the initial listing of Shem, Ham, and Japheth (10:1) is consistent with their first mention in Genesis 5:32, the genealogy takes a turn by unpacking Japheth's family line first (10:2–5), then moving on to Ham (10:6–20) and Shem (10:21–31).

Japheth's family line is the least developed genealogy and thus the most challenging to interpret. Some scholars believe Japheth's descendants were allies of Israel. Genesis 9:27 describes Japheth sharing the tents of Shem, hinting that they shared the land. Meanwhile, other scholars believe Japheth's line traces to the Philistines, who eventually competed against the Israelites for land and power.

Ham's family line centers on Canaan and the political and theological effects of the curse. While Shem and Japheth are blessed, Canaan is cursed, pointing toward the power struggle between Israel and Canaan that will unfold for years to come.

Shem's line leads intentionally and directly to Abraham. Ten generations are listed between Shem and Abraham, the same number of generations listed between Adam and Noah in Genesis 5. These genealogies take on new significance in Luke 3:34–38 when the lineage of Jesus is traced back to Shem, Noah, and Adam.

The genealogy details many territories, clans, nations, and languages, hinting that the people are becoming diverse in their geography, ethnicity, communication, and culture.

One of the most interesting characters in the genealogy is Nimrod, the grandson of Ham, whose name means "we shall rebel." Genesis 10:8 tells us that his name fit his aggressive reputation. He was known as a tyrant. Rather than build altars to God, he built cities. His empire included all of Mesopotamia. Nimrod is noted for founding the godless cities of Babylon and Nineveh. Years later, these cities bring Israel to her knees, yet even here we are reminded that nothing is beyond the reach of God's redemptive plan.

As people multiply, they move — some head to the coast, others settle inland. Overall, the genealogy highlights God's ongoing blessing to be fruitful, multiply, and fill the earth (Genesis 9:1).

2. Read Genesis 11. As the people journey east, they settle on a plain in Shinar (11:2). This is not the first time people are described as moving eastward. What role does "east" play in each of the following passages?

Genesis 3:24:

Genesis 4:16:

What kinds of situations tempt you to head "east" rather than toward a closer, more intimate relationship with God?

After the flood, people settle in southern Mesopotamia where the building materials are different than those in Israel or Egypt. Any stones in the area had to be carried in at great expense and labor. Thus, the people turn to bricks for their most valuable buildings.

The region was also known for its ziggurats, massive monuments that resemble pyramids, which were dedicated to various deities. The main architectural features of a ziggurat are a stairway or ramp that leads to the top of the building and a small area at the top of the structure — a guest room — to accommodate the god. A ziggurat was built to make it easier for a deity to descend, accept worship, and bless the people. This may have been what the people had in mind when they dreamed up their construction project.

3. Why do you think God took offense at people building a tower?

What are some examples of offensive towers people still build today; in other words, specific ways we try to manipulate or replace God?

4. How many times does the phrase "let us" appear in Genesis 11:4?

What does this phrase reveal about the people's focus?

What happens in your own life when you shift your focus away from God?

The people want to penetrate divinity in order to lay hold of divinity themselves. The people build a tower with the expectation that God will come down, and when he does, it's not with the response they had hoped. God recognizes that people have crossed a threshold of corruption and sin which cannot be undone. Humanity refuses to live within its God-given boundaries.

5. In what ways are the people struggling to live within their God-given boundaries?

In what ways do you struggle to live within God-given boundaries?

Rather than ban the building of future towers or send a plague on the builders, God cuts to the heart of the issue: he confuses the people's language. The result is that cooperation is impossible and scattering becomes inevitable. The place is named Babel, meaning "confusion," which sounds like the Hebrew word for Babylon.

The story of the tower of Babel carries poetic beauty and irony. The story begins with all the earth speaking one language and ends with everyone speaking different languages. The people who want to make a name for themselves end up with the name "confusion."

Throughout the book of Genesis, sin and corruption find new outlets and expressions:

*   Adam and Eve choose to eat the forbidden fruit in an effort to be like God.
*   Cain falls into temptation and murders his brother because God did not regard his offering.
*   Before the flood, people are overcome by evil in their minds and actions.
*   After the flood, humankind tries to build its own path to God's presence.

Before Genesis 11 comes to a close, we are offered a final genealogy of Shem, one of Noah's sons. This is the genealogy that links Noah to Abraham and sets the scene for Abraham's unique calling by God: he will father a nation that will bless the nations.

6. Reflecting on the first eleven chapters of Genesis, what have you learned about the nature of God and God's loving care for humanity and creation?

Spend some time prayerfully considering any offensive towers that you may have built in your own life. Ask the Holy Spirit to illuminate any areas where you may be depending on yourself rather than God. Ask for forgiveness and the grace and strength to tear down those towers and humbly depend on God.

DAY FIVE: The Challenges of Choosing to Believe
Genesis 12

Abraham's journey is filled with highs and lows with a few loop-de-loops thrown in. God uses an infertile couple to fill the earth with people who are called to know and love the Creator. Nearly everything that happens in the life of Abraham traces back to the first three verses of Genesis 12. The highlights and lowlights of his journey either demonstrate a movement toward the fulfillment of these promises and blessings or an obstacle diverting Abraham away from them.

1. Read Genesis 12:1–3. God's call on Abraham in this passage contains seven elements, which is the symbolic number for totality or completeness. Use the chart to identify the seven elements of God's covenant with Abraham.

The seven elements of God's covenant with Abraham
1. *make of him a great nation*
2. *bless him*
3. *make his name great*

The seven elements of God's covenant with Abraham	
4.	he will be a blessing
5.	bless those who bless him
6.	curse those who curse him
7.	all communities of the earth shall find blessing in him.

Abraham probably never expected the Promised Land to be full of famine. Rather than call out to God about how to handle the situation, Abraham decides to travel to Egypt. While most areas depend on rainfall for their water, Egypt depends on the annual flooding of the Nile, making it less susceptible to famine than other areas. It's worth noting that Abraham doesn't build a single altar along the way, an indication that seeking God doesn't mark his journey.

2. Read Genesis 12:4–20. God promises Abraham land, but instead of laying hold of the land, Abraham is confronted with famine. When have you experienced God leading you into a situation that was different than you expected?

How did your response compare to Abraham's?

After arriving in Egypt, Abraham deceives the authorities. Abraham and Sarah barely escape with their lives. The story of Abraham in Egypt foreshadows the story of God's people in Egypt centuries later.

3. The Scripture passages in the following chart compare the story of Abraham to other stories in the Old Testament. Use the space provided to note the parallels between these stories and Abraham's story.

Scriptures	Parallels
Genesis 12:10 and Genesis 47:4	
Genesis 12:12–15 and Exodus 1:11–14	
Genesis 12:17 and Exodus 7:14–12:30	
Genesis 12:16 and Exodus 12:33–36	

How does paying attention to parallels between stories enhance your appreciation of Scripture and deepen your understanding of God's Word?

4. After all God had done to protect and provide for Abraham — defeating kings, rescuing Lot, instituting the covenant of circumcision — Abraham still thinks he needs to take matters into his own hands. What mental arguments do you imagine Abraham used to justify the deception?

Have you ever taken matters into your own hands and chosen deception rather than honesty? What was the result?

Spend some time prayerfully considering if there are any areas of dishonesty in your life which you need to confess. Ask God for wisdom on how to best handle the situation.

The Pursuit, the Promise, and the Provision

Genesis 12–23

Although I don't know the tantalizing details that surrounded Abraham's launch into the adventure of knowing God, it's clear that something stirred in his heart. The small candle of his conscience must have been lit, his spirit must have sought to draw near to the one true living God, because God leaned out of heaven and invaded Abraham's life.[8]

–Anne Graham Lotz

Faith isn't easy. Faith asks us to respond to divine direction rather than just the observable data. Faith invites us to embrace the goodness of God even when what we see around us suggests God doesn't have our best interests at heart. Faith asks us to resist taking matters into our own hands. Faith challenges us to believe the impossible. And faith asks us to live courageously, abandoning ourselves to God's care.

Abraham (early in his story known as Abram) chooses to embark on an unforgettable journey of faith. Through Abraham's story, we discover much about God. We learn how God pursues even the most unlikely people with unfathomable love. We discover that God remains true to his promises even when we fumble and stumble. And we watch as God provides — at times in the most unexpected and outrageous ways. Abraham's story illuminates what it means to respond to the God who pursues us.

Getting Started: Select One

Experiential Activity: The Promise of God to Abraham

What you'll need:

- ◆ Hubble Telescope images of discoveries from space
- ◆ Photocopies of the images or a laptop and video projector to display the images

1. Visit websites such as *www.hubblesite.org* or check out books from the local library to find breathtaking images taken by the Hubble Telescope.* If you have access to a projector, the wallpaper gallery at *www.hubblesite.org/gallery/wallpaper* provides a spectacular collection.
2. Share these images with the group and then read Romans 1:20.
3. Discuss the following questions:

   - In what ways does nature display the invisible attributes of God?
   - How does God reveal himself through nature?
   - Imagine yourself as Abraham looking up at the sky and the stars above as God promised countless descendants (Genesis 15:5). What do you think Abraham felt as he listened to God's promise?
   - How do you think God continued to use quiet, star-filled nights to remind Abraham of divine faithfulness throughout Abraham's life?

   *Be sure to note if there are any restrictions on duplicating the image or if it is necessary to secure permission to reproduce the image.

Icebreaker Question

If you're not doing the experiential activity, choose one *of the following questions to begin your discussion.*

- When you meet someone for the first time, who is the person you're most commonly associated with? (for example: *You might be introduced as Mary's mom, Bob's boss, Karen's friend, Luke's brother, Pat's spouse.*) How does it make you feel to be so closely linked to this person?
- In what ways have you specifically sensed God pursuing you?
- Imagine God asking you, like Abraham, to leave everything that's familiar to travel to another part of the world. How would you feel about leaving everything and everyone you know and love?

Three: The Pursuit, the Promise, and the Provision

As you watch the DVD, use the following outline to take notes on anything that stands out to you.

Not only does Abraham* not know God, but he isn't exactly a prime candidate to be chosen.

Abraham's life story is testament that God is true. Despite mistakes and setbacks, God fulfills all the promises.

God "pursues" — Abraham

God doesn't take away anything from Abraham that isn't replaced.

To serve the God of Abraham means that we also serve a God who pursues, promises, and provides.

God "makes" + "provides" promises

---

*For ease of use, Margaret uses the names Abraham and Sarah, though they are first known as Abram and Sarai.

Abraham's story reminds us that no matter where we are, even if we're living in the land of Ur, a place representative of serving false gods, a place marked by loss, pain, and poor choices, God pursues us there.

 ## Group Discussion Questions

1. Consider what you learned about the pursuit, promises, and provision of God from the Afterhours personal studies or on the DVD. What caught your attention or stood out most to you?

> **Quotable**
>
> "Ur belonged to the moon god (incidentally, called Sin). The Sumerians could boast of running water and the beginning of a written alphabet. Abram and his people could have enjoyed a pleasant and rather uneventful life there in the Fertile Crescent."[9]
> –Celia Brewer Sinclair, author and lecturer

The Pursuit of God

2. God chooses Abraham — a man who doesn't know God from a coconut — to be the father of our faith. What encouragement do you find in God's selection of Abraham?

3. Do you tend to think of your own spiritual life in terms of God pursuing you or of you pursuing God? Why?

4. In what specific ways have you experienced God pursuing you recently?

The Promises of God

5. Read Genesis 12:1 – 3. How do you think you would respond if God asked of you the same thing he asked of Abraham?

6. Which of God's promises to Abraham is one you would like to claim as your own right now? Why?

7. The calling of Abraham and the promise God gives him hinge on a ruthless abandonment of what is familiar and comfortable. In what ways has God called you to abandon what is familiar and comfortable?

8. The story of Abraham raises important questions about faith:

    In what or in whom do you place your faith?

    What do you have faith for?

What shakes your faith?

What strengthens your faith?

Quotable

"Why and how does one continue to trust solely in the promise when the evidence against the promise is all around? It is the scandal that is forced here. It is Abraham's embrace of this scandal that makes him the father of faith."[10]

–Walter Brueggemann

The Provision of God

9. When in the last six months have you experienced God providing for you or your family in a specific, meaningful way? In what way does God's provision demonstrate God's love for you?

10. In your own words, what does it mean to serve the God of Abraham?

The story of Abraham is a reminder that the journey of faith is paved with uncertainty. Yet that is the journey to which God calls us — one that is marked by the pursuit, the promises, and the provision of God.

Close in Prayer

Ask God to:

- Provide a deeper understanding of the depths of love God has for you.
- Bring to mind any specific promises God had given you in the past.
- Strengthen your faith.

 ## Jumpstart

To get an insider's look at the Pursuing God series, bonus features, and freebies, as well as join the online discussion, visit *www.pursuinggodbiblestudy.com*.

To prepare for the next session, read Genesis 24–27 and tackle the After-hours personal studies.

Afterhours Personal Studies

Dive deeper into the book of Genesis by engaging in these five personal studies. If you only have time for one, choose Day Five, which will prepare you specifically for the next session.

DAY ONE: Tests and Trials of the Faith Journey
Genesis 13–15

Though famine creates problems for Abraham while in Egypt, tensions now soar as a result of abundance. Abraham is not only rich, but *very* rich with all his livestock, silver, and gold. With so much wealth, conflict breaks out among the herdsmen who serve Abraham and Lot. There simply aren't enough natural resources to sustain all their animals in one place.

1. Read Genesis 13. For Abraham and Lot, the issues of abundance and scarcity lead to conflict. How has scarcity led to conflict in your life?

    How has abundance led to conflict in your life?

2. Abraham seeks to be a peacemaker in the sticky situation with the herdsmen. What sacrifice does Abraham make to keep the peace (Genesis 13:8–9)?

    Have you ever made a sacrifice in order to keep the peace in a relationship? Was it worth it? Why or why not?

Though Lot chooses the best land, God still promises to give Abraham the land. God instructs Abraham to walk the land as a symbol of his acquisition of the property. In response to God's renewed promises, Abraham builds an altar.

In the wake of Abraham's generous peacemaking effort with Lot, conflict arises in the surrounding territories. War breaks out among the kings and Lot is taken hostage.

Throughout Genesis 14, the word "king" appears twenty-eight times. Though there are five kings of Canaan and four kings of Mesopotamia, as well as Melchizedek, king of Salem, we are reminded that there's only one true king — God, who rules over all.

3. Read Genesis 14. Abraham makes the decision to show loyalty to his disloyal nephew. Have you ever shown loyalty to someone who has been disloyal to you? What was the result?

4. The king of Salem, a place some scholars believe to be Jerusalem (Psalm 76:2), and the king of Sodom take different approaches when dealing with Abraham. How does the king of Salem greet Abraham (Genesis 14:18–20)?

How does the king of Sodom greet Abraham (Genesis 14:21)?

How are their greetings reflective of the land and people they lead?

5. When you think about the attitudes you display toward others, do you tend to have the attitude of the king of Salem or the king of Sodom? Why?

What situations tend to bring out each attitude in you?

Abraham refuses the plunder offered to him by the king of Sodom. Though it's rightly his, Abraham knows that if he takes the booty, the presumptuous king will forever claim he made Abraham rich. God comes to Abraham in a vision and promises to be his protector and reward.

In Genesis 15, Abraham notes that despite all of God's promises and provision, he and Sarah are still childless. God assures Abraham that he will have a child from his own body. But that's not all!

After asking Abraham to admire the stars in the sky, God reminds him that God is the one who has brought him out of Ur and will give him the land. Abraham is skeptical. Why? Possibly because the promise isn't just about being given the land; it also means those who are in the land will have to be removed. Abraham asks God how he can know for sure the land will be his. God doesn't blink at the request. Instead, God enters into a covenant with Abraham in which God is the only responsible party.

God asks Abraham to bring a heifer, a goat, a ram, a turtledove, and a pigeon, and cut each animal in two. That evening the Lord appears as a smoking firepot and torch—images of purification—and passes between the pieces, establishing a covenant with Abraham.

Notable

Genesis 15:17 describes a smoking cooking pot passing between the two halves of each animal. In the Bible, smoke, fire, and flames are often representative of God's presence. Consider Exodus 3:1–6, Exodus 19:16–18, and Revelation 1:12–16.

6. Read Genesis 15. Abraham's faith is renewed, but as the father of faith he is still living on the promises of God. What kinds of promises are you waiting for God to fulfill in your own life?

How has waiting shaped your:

Personal growth ...

Faith ...

Relationship with God ...

Spend some time reflecting on the promises God has made to you through the Scriptures. Thank God for the divine promises and the faithfulness displayed in your life.

DAY TWO: The Blessings and Judgments of God
Genesis 16–18

Despite God's presence, provision, and the covenant promise of descendants, Abraham believes the only way he's going to get a son is to take matters into his own hands. Rather than listen to God's voice, he listens to the voice of his wife and agrees to sleep with her maid Hagar, whose name can be translated "forsaken." The result is Ishmael.

1. Read Genesis 16. In what ways did Hagar get shortchanged for her service to Sarah and Abraham?

What does God's response to Hagar reveal about the nature of God (Genesis 16:9–11; 21:13–18)?

He protected her and Ishmael.

At the age of ninety-nine, Abraham—still called Abram—is visited by God again. God renews the promise and also gives Abram and Sarai their new names. Abram becomes Abraham, meaning "father of many." Sarai is the only woman in the Bible whose name is changed. She becomes Sarah, which can be translated as "princess."

2. Read Genesis 17. God makes a covenant with Abraham that can be divided into three parts—one for God, one for Abraham, and one for Sarah. Use the following chart to write down the main points of the covenant for each party.

Responsible party	Introduction	Scripture	Covenant obligations
God	"As for me"	Genesis 17:4–8	
Abraham	"As for you"	Genesis 17:9–14	
Sarah	"As for Sarah"	Genesis 17:15–16	

What one or two things make it difficult for you to walk blamelessly with God as Abraham did?

After establishing the covenant, God asks Abraham to be circumcised. Circumcision is a sign of being set apart. The male sex organ that enables God's people to have descendants is purified and set apart for God. The choice is permanent and irreversible.

While physical circumcision is crucial to God's covenant with Abraham, it is only a representation of a deeper issue—circumcision of the heart. God wants our hearts to be set apart for him. Scripture often makes reference to a circumcised heart or the idea that the Holy Spirit now writes the law of God on our hearts.

3. What do the following passages reveal about what it means to have our hearts circumcised to God?

Ezekiel 44:7–9:

Jeremiah 31:31–34:

Romans 2:28–29:

Galatians 6:15:

In what ways has your own heart been circumcised to God?

In Genesis 18, Abraham has two significant spiritual encounters in which he discovers the realities of the blessings and judgments of God. Abraham shows hospitality to three men who aren't your ordinary visitors. Then, Abraham has an encounter with God in which he pleads on behalf of Sodom.

4. Read Genesis 18. Why do you think Sarah laughed at the news of the angels?

Who else laughed at the promise of a child (Genesis 17:17)?

Have you ever laughed at something God promised you? If so, describe.

Notable

The word for "outcry" found in Genesis 18:20–21 and 19:13 can be translated "outrage" and finds its roots in the anguished cry of the oppressed, the plea of a victim who has experienced injustice.

5. God approaches Abraham to discuss the fate of Sodom and Gomorrah. How do each of the following parties benefit from the discussion:

God . . .

Abraham . . .

Lot and his family . . .

The people of Sodom and Gomorrah . . .

6. In what ways does Genesis 18:1 – 15, 18 – 19 reveal the blessing of God?

In what ways does Genesis 18:20 – 33 reveal the judgments of God?

In what ways have you seen or experienced the blessings and judgments of God revealed in the last six months?

Spend some time reflecting on both the blessings and judgments of God in your own life. Thank God for both the blessing and judgments and the way they beckon you into a more intimate relationship with God.

DAY THREE: Lessons from Lot and Abraham
Genesis 19–20

Following God's conversation with Abraham, two angels visit Sodom. When the angels enter the city, Lot is sitting at the city gate. In ancient cultures, the city gate was a symbol of authority and governing power. Lot's presence at the gate suggests he has some form of political authority in the city.

1. Read Genesis 19. How does Abraham's hospitality toward his visitors (Genesis 18:3 – 8) compare with the hospitality of Lot and Sodom (Genesis 19:1 – 10)?

Is the hospitality that you offer others more like Abraham's or Lot's?

2. While the sexual sin of Sodom is highlighted in Genesis 19, other passages
   of Scripture reveal additional sins committed by the inhabitants of the
   city. Use the chart to note what each passage reveals about Sodom's sins.

Scripture	Sodom's sins
Isaiah 1:10–17	
Jeremiah 23:14	
Ezekiel 16:49	

Reflecting on these passages and reputation of the city, which of the sins
of Sodom do you tend to struggle with the most?

Lot is now in a lose-lose situation. If he hands over his guests to the mob
outside his door, they'll be raped and abused. Lot chooses to do the unthinkable;
he offers his own daughters in their place. Some scholars believe that Lot's desire
to save his guests — and not act as selfishly as the rest of Sodom — is what saves
both him and his daughters.

A bit of irony is found in Lot's request to go to Zoar (Genesis 19:18–19).
Zoar can be translated "small." Lot has been transformed from loving the big
city to desiring a small town where he can get away.

3. What parallels do you find between the story of Lot and the story of Noah? Use the chart to note your observations.

Scriptures	Similarities between Lot and Noah
Genesis 6:13 and Genesis 19:13	
Genesis 6:8–9 and Genesis 19:12–13	
Genesis 7:6 and Genesis 19:24	
Genesis 7:16 and Genesis 19:10	
Genesis 9:22 and Genesis 19:32	
Genesis 6:5–8 and Genesis 19:29	

What surprises you about the similarities between these two men? Do you relate more to Lot or Noah? Why?

4. Read Genesis 20. The story of Abraham in Egypt (Genesis 12:10–20) parallels the story of Abraham in Gerar (Genesis 20:1–8). What are the
 • differences and similarities between the two stories?

5. One of the ironies captured in Genesis 20 is that Abimelek fears God more than Abraham does. In fact, here Abraham fears people more than he does God. In what areas of your life are you tempted to fear other people more than you fear God?

What temptations or failures do you find yourself wrestling with again and again?

Spend some time asking God to give you strength to resist any temptations that you face on an ongoing basis. Pray that God will send people around you who strengthen you, encourage you, and hold you accountable in a healthy and vibrant way.

DAY FOUR: Ultimate Faith

Genesis 21–23

After years of waiting, the promised heir is born. Abraham names his son Isaac, as the angels instructed, and then circumcises him, as God instructed. The child whose name means "laughter" is now a source of laughter and joy for his parents.

The thrill of the moment does not last long as Sarah turns her eyes toward her maidservant, Hagar, and her son. Throughout Genesis 21, Ishmael's name is never mentioned; he is referred to only as "her son" and "the boy." This suggests Ishmael's secondary status to Isaac.

1. Read Genesis 21:1–21. The birth of Isaac opens up a blister of anger and resentment in Sarah toward Hagar and Ishmael. Hagar runs away. Stranded in the desert without water, she chooses to leave her child to die,

but God intervenes — sending an angel and renewing the divine promise to her. Consider an area of your life or a difficult relationship that is so broken or hard it seems beyond help. How do you hope God might renew you or your relationship in a meaningful way?

In Galatians, Paul contrasts the faith of Hagar and Ishmael with the faith of Sarah and Isaac. Hagar and Ishmael are likened to the human effort to keep the laws of Judaism while Sarah and Isaac are likened to the promise and grace of God.

> **Notable**
>
> The skin of water Abraham sent with Hagar into the desert would have held approximately three gallons.

2. Read Galatians 4:21 – 31. Use the following chart to note the areas of contrast between Hagar and Sarah.

Scripture	Hagar	Sarah
Ex.: Galatians 4:23	Ex.: Bondwoman	Ex.: Freewoman

Reflecting on your own spiritual journey, do you tend to feel more like a child from the seed of Hagar or the seed of Sarah? Why?

Genesis 22 is one of the most challenging passages in the Bible. Everything God promises Abraham hinges on Isaac, yet God asks Abraham to sacrifice his own son. Abraham binds not only his son, but also the promises of God to the altar, and is willing to let them die. This scene reveals that Abraham had come to a place of being wholly surrendered to God.

3. Read Genesis 22. If God asked you to bind the most precious thing in your life to the altar, what would it be?

God does, in fact, ask us to surrender everything to him. What thoughts or emotions are you aware of when you consider the implications of surrendering the people or things that are most precious to you?

4. The story of Isaac and the story of Jesus share many of the same characteristics. Use the following chart to note the scriptural parallels between the two.

Passages	Parallels between Isaac and Jesus
Genesis 17:16 and Luke 1:31	
Genesis 17:19 and Matthew 1:21	
Genesis 18:10–15 and Matthew 1:1	
Genesis 18:12 and Luke 1:7	
Genesis 21:2 and Galatians 4:4	

Passages	Parallels between Isaac and Jesus
Genesis 22:2 and John 1:14; 3:16	
Genesis 22:2 and Matthew 26:39	
Genesis 22:6 and John 19:17	
Genesis 22:9 and Matthew 27:2	
Hebrews 11:17 – 19 and 1 Corinthians 15:4	
Genesis 22:4 and Matthew 12:40	
Genesis 25:5 and Hebrews 1:2	
Genesis 24:67 and Ephesians 5:25	

Which parallels between Isaac and Christ are most meaningful to you? Why?

The exchange between Abraham and Ephron in Genesis 23 over what to pay for a parcel of land is somewhat reminiscent of two people arguing about who will pick up the tab for dinner. Both men are wealthy and the sum of money is insignificant to Abraham, yet the tension persists.

> **Notable**
>
> In Genesis 23:6, the Hittites call Abraham "mighty prince" or "prince of God." Though Abraham doesn't own any land in Canaan, they recognize God's blessing, provision, and protection on his life.

5. Read Genesis 23. The parcel Abraham purchases for Sarah's burial will be the only piece of the Promised Land he will own before his death. Though Ephron calls the 400 pieces of silver a small portion, his asking price is high; yet Abraham chooses to pay the full amount. Abraham refuses to receive the land as a gift, in part so that Ephron's heirs cannot reclaim it after Ephron dies. What does Abraham's concern for Sarah's burial—its location as well as its details—reveal about his care for her?

It's worth noting that the author of Genesis chooses to tell the story of Abraham immediately after the stories of the flood and tower of Babel. By arranging the stories in this way, the author reveals the fallen nature of humanity and then gives us great hope that God is still faithful and engaged in the world. God has a plan for humanity and the redemptive plan will continue to unfold. Even the sinfulness of God's people cannot thwart God's love.

Spend some time prayerfully considering anything in your life that God may want you to give up. Sometimes God asks us to give something up because it's sinful or a distraction in our lives. But sometimes it's for another reason. Isaac's story reveals that occasionally God asks us to give something up to ensure that we hold nothing else as precious as God, even if it's something good God gives us. Prayerfully reflect on any activities, relationships, commitments, or goals that you need to lay down in order to lay hold of God more fully.

God has been faithful to Abraham. Through a series of miraculous events, Isaac is born. In a place known as "The LORD Will Provide" or "Yahweh-jireh," Abraham is asked to sacrifice his own son. At the last moment, an angel intervenes and Isaac's life is spared. Yet for the promises of God to unfold in Abraham's life, Isaac must find a wife and have children of his own.

1. Read Genesis 24:1 – 14. Why do you think it was important to Abraham that his future daughter-in-law not be from among the Canaanites (Genesis 9:24 – 27) but from his homeland? (*Hint:* See Genesis 12:1 – 3.)

Notable

Oaths in the ancient world varied greatly. The image of placing a hand under another person's thigh (24:2, 9) implies making an oath at the source of life (genitalia), which is poignant considering this oath involves Abraham's descendants.

Abraham's servant will be released from his commitment to bring back a bride if the woman herself is unwilling to follow him to Canaan. This exception suggests Abraham is moving forward by faith rather than presumption or force. Abraham recognizes the importance of the woman's choice and knows that if this is from God, then she will be willing to leave her homeland.

The servant's prayer for God's guidance in finding Isaac's future wife begins and ends with a request for God to show loving-kindness to Abraham. The Hebrew word for "kindness" is *hesed* and implies a loyalty to a covenant relationship. It's also worth noting that this is the first prayer in the Bible asking for specific guidance. Isaac and Rebekah's meeting is bathed in prayer.

2. Read Genesis 24:15 – 28. God answers the prayer of Abraham's servant before he even finishes speaking it. Have you ever had God answer one of your prayers before you finished? If so, describe in the space below.

Overall, how would you describe your experience of God's timing in responding to your prayers? Place an X on the continuum to indicate your response.

———————————————————————————————

GOD RESPONDS TO MY
PRAYERS QUICKLY.

GOD RESPONDS TO MY
PRAYERS SLOWLY.

Overall, how responsive do you feel God is to your prayers? Place an X on the continuum to indicate your response.

———————————————————————————————

GOD IS NOT VERY RESPONSIVE
TO MY PRAYERS.

GOD IS VERY RESPONSIVE
TO MY PRAYERS.

How does your perception of God's timing and responsiveness to your prayers affect how you pray?

Rebekah's name can be translated "ensnaring beauty," and she's noted for her outer appearance as well as for being a virgin. She is an adolescent girl of marrying age and seems like an ideal selection for Isaac, but the real test will take place at the well (Genesis 24:15–16).

3. In what ways did Rebekah and her act of service at the well exceed the servant's request to God?

When was the last time God's answer to your prayers exceeded your expectations?

How did the experience affect your prayer life and relationship with God?

Rebekah shares that she's the daughter of Bethuel, the son of Milcah. This is significant for the servant and Abraham. Bethuel is Isaac's cousin, so the divine providence of meeting Rebekah at the well far exceeds all the servant's expectations. Before the servant follows Rebekah back to her family's house, he takes a moment to pray and thank God.

The servant is a highly effective communicator who uses precise and persuasive language. The servant appeals to Laban's greed by describing Abraham's wealth and making it clear that Isaac is the only heir. Because Isaac will not marry among the Canaanites, Rebekah's heirs will be sole heirs. The servant shares the details of God's providence and appeals to the covenant with Abraham. In response, Laban acknowledges God's divine hand and agrees to allow Rebekah to make the journey with the servant and to marry Isaac.

4. Read Genesis 24:29–60. What is the servant's response to Laban (v. 52)?

How do you imagine your life might be different if it were marked by prayer?

The moment Isaac and Rebekah meet unfolds like a scene in a classic romantic movie. Rebekah is brave enough to leave everything except for a few maids and supplies to travel to an unknown land. Abraham made a similar journey years earlier.

5. Read Genesis 24:61–67. What do you imagine Rebekah felt as she left her family and homeland?

6. Rebekah takes a huge risk by leaving almost everything she owns to travel to a foreign land to marry an unknown man. Through her act of faith, she becomes part of a family line that will bless the entire world. What risk might God be asking you to take as an act of faith?

What do you imagine the blessing of taking the risk might be?

Isaac takes Rebekah into his mother's tent. As Isaac's wife, Rebekah is now the head woman of the household. Abraham is likely thrilled at the news of the arrival of his future daughter-in-law.

Spend some time reflecting on the risks God has been calling you to take in your own life. Ask God for the courage and strength to respond bravely and obediently.

Ida Mae's - great nephew Daniel
     - niece Sharon
Craig - healing
Gloria - chemo
Fritz' marriage
Carol's grandsons marriage

When Love Goes Right and When Love Goes Wrong

Genesis 24–27

> Christian Love, either towards God or towards man, is an affair of the will. If we are trying to do His will we are obeying the commandment, "Thou shalt love the Lord thy God." He will give us feelings of love if He pleases. We cannot create them for ourselves, and we must not demand them as a right. But the great thing to remember is that, though our feelings come and go, His love for us does not.[13]
>
> −C. S. Lewis

One of the many reasons I love Scripture is its captivating storytelling. Whether it's Eve facing off with a serpent in the garden or Noah staying afloat on the ark, the Bible is full of adventure. The pages are also laced with drama in stories such as Sarah vying with Hagar or the competition between Leah and Rachel. And there are stories of love: men and women who choose to love God wholeheartedly, as well as sparkling romances.

Two of the patriarchs, Abraham and Isaac, challenge us to consider what it means to love God and love others — not just for today or tomorrow but for a lifetime — and what it means to finish well.

Experiential Activity: Heart Collage

What you'll need:
- ◆ A large piece of poster board
- ◆ Superglue
- ◆ Red and/or white construction paper
- ◆ Colored markers
- ◆ Scissors

1. Provide each participant with a sheet of red and/or white paper, a pair of scissors, and a marker.
2. Invite everyone to cut out paper hearts. On each heart, write the name of something or someone you love. Be creative! Have fun!
3. Once all the hearts are created, invite participants to share what they wrote on their hearts and why.
4. Glue all of the hearts onto the poster board to make a collage.
5. Email a picture of your collage to *info@margaretfeinberg.com* and it may be posted on her site!

Icebreaker Question

If you're not doing the experiential activity, choose one *of the following questions to begin your discussion.*

- When you think about a great love story, which books or movies come to mind?
- What are some of the characteristics of a great love story?
- When you think about romantic love stories from the Bible, which ones do you think of?

God Is Able - Priscilla Schiar
Becoming A Woman of Symplicity -
                        Cynthia Heald

Four: When Love Goes Right and When Love Goes Wrong

As you watch the DVD, use the following outline to take notes on anything that stands out to you.

Relationships aren't easy. Sometimes they get messy. Miscommunication occurs. Misunderstandings happen. Mistakes are made. Before we know it, a relationship we celebrated and treasured falls apart.

Abraham is a man whose life is marked by faith. He orients his life, his family, his everything on the promises of God. Meanwhile, Sarah is a woman whose body is transformed from barrenness into birthing a nation because of the power and promise of God.

Despite a wondrous beginning, a match made in heaven, Isaac and Rebekah's faith journeys and life together turn out much differently than one would expect. Rather than being a story of when love goes right, it quickly becomes a story of when love goes wrong.

Rebekah isn't given a memorial in Scripture, only a passing mention in Genesis 49 that she's buried alongside Isaac in the same place as Abraham and Sarah. To be a patriarch's wife and not be given a memorial in Genesis means you did not finish well.

Bottom line: Those who begin well do not always finish well.

My prayer for you is that God will give you the strength and courage to choose wisely today so that you may finish well, like Abraham, blessed and loved by God and those who know you best.

ᴉᴴᴉ Group Discussion Questions

(30–45 MINUTES)

1. Consider what you learned about divine and romantic love from the After-hours personal studies or on the DVD. What caught your attention or stood out most to you?

When Love Goes Right

2. Without naming anyone specific, describe a friendship in your life that exemplifies when "love goes right." What are some of the characteristics of that relationship? (example: *honesty, consistent communication*)

3. Read Genesis 22:2–12. Based on this passage, what three to five words or phrases would you use to describe Abraham's love for God? (example: *sacrificial*)

4. To what degree would you say these same characteristics describe your love for God? A little, a lot, or somewhere in between? Place an X on the continuum to indicate your response. Then, if you feel comfortable, share the reasons for your response.

THE CHARACTERISTICS OF
ABRAHAM'S LOVE FOR GOD
DO NOT AT ALL DESCRIBE
MY LOVE FOR GOD.

THE CHARACTERISTICS OF
ABRAHAM'S LOVE FOR GOD
COMPLETELY DESCRIBE
MY LOVE FOR GOD.

5. Read Genesis 23:1–9. What does this passage reveal about Abraham's love for Sarah?

6. Do you know anyone whose relationship shares characteristics with Abraham and Sarah's? If so, briefly describe. What is it you admire most about this couple? If you can't think of anyone, why do you think this kind of relationship might be so rare?

When Love Goes Wrong

7. Without naming anyone specific, describe a friendship in your life that exemplifies when "love goes wrong."

What issues caused the relationship to sour? (example: *lack of communication*)

8. Read Genesis 25:27–28; 27:1–13. What do you think contributed to the deterioration of Isaac and Rebekah's relationship?

What kind of tension does deception create in a relationship? A family?

What are the fruits of deception? (example: *mistrust*)

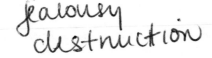
jealousy
destruction

Finishing Well

9. On the DVD, Margaret says, "Those who begin well do not always finish well. And those who do not begin well do not have to end that way." Overall, would you say your current spiritual trajectory is leading you to become more like Abraham or Isaac? Place an X on the continuum to indicate your response. Then, if you feel comfortable, share the reasons for your response.

MY SPIRITUAL TRAJECTORY IS LEADING ME TO BECOME MORE LIKE ISAAC.	MY SPIRITUAL TRAJECTORY IS LEADING ME TO BECOME MORE LIKE ABRAHAM.

10. Margaret describes rebuilding her relationship with Carly. What thoughts or emotions are you aware of when you consider the possibility of taking steps to rebuild a broken relationship in your own life?

The love stories of Abraham and Sarah as well as Isaac and Rebekah remind us that in our lives we have some relationships in which love goes right and others in which love goes wrong. But as God's children we can make choices to make them right! This is true not only in our romantic relationships but also in our friendships and in our relationship with God.

Close in Prayer

Ask God to:

- Illuminate any relationships that need restoration and healing.
- Bless and strengthen the relationships you've been given.
- Give you strength and tenacity to finish well in your own spiritual journey.

Jumpstart

To get an insider's look at the Pursuing God series, bonus features, and freebies, as well as join the online discussion, visit *www.pursuinggodbiblestudy.com*.

To prepare for the next session, read Genesis 28–36 and tackle the After-hours personal studies.

Afterhours Personal Studies

Dive deeper into the book of Genesis by engaging in these five personal studies. If you only have time for one, choose Day Five, which will prepare you specifically for the next session.

DAY ONE: Reflecting on Abraham's Life

Genesis 25:1–18

Abraham's life story comes to a close with the news that Abraham has taken another wife, Keturah, whose name means "incense" or "enveloped in fragrant smoke." Keturah's role is unclear because in Genesis 25:1 she is called a wife but in Genesis 25:6 she is referred to as a concubine. She may have become a full wife sometime during her life with Abraham. Abraham's kindness and generosity is displayed again before his death. Though he is not required to give anything to sons born to concubines, he chooses to show generosity anyway.

1. Read Genesis 25:1 – 11. Why do you think Abraham chooses to give his sons gifts when he is only required to give Isaac the full share of his inheritance?

    What does Abraham's generosity reveal about his own character? His relationship with God?

    In what ways do your actions display your inner character?

> **Notable**
>
> Keturah bore Abraham six sons, the most notable of whom is Midian. Midian's descendants, the Midianites, make several appearances in the Scripture. Joseph is transported to Egypt by Midianite traders (Genesis 37:28) and Moses marries into a family headed by the priest of Midian named Jethro (Exodus 3:1; Numbers 10:29). The Midianites partake in the disaster at Baal Peor along with the Moabites, and Moses orders their extermination in Numbers 31.

2. How is Abraham described before his death in Genesis 25:7–8?

   How is this description a fulfillment of God's promise? (*Hint:* See Genesis 15:15.)

   How would you like to be described when you're at the same stage of life as Abraham?

3. Abraham's story is reflected on throughout both the Old Testament and the New Testament. Look up the following passages, then use the chart to note what each one reveals about Abraham. Place a checkmark next to any of the statements that might be true of you right now.

Scripture	Insight about Abraham	✓
2 Chronicles 20:7		
Isaiah 29:22		
Matthew 1:1–16		
John 8:56		

What insights did you discover in considering how your life is similar to or different from the descriptions of Abraham's life?

4. Reflecting on what you've learned so far, sum up the life of Abraham in ten words or less.

5. Read Genesis 25:12–18. Isaac and Ishmael bury Abraham next to Sarah. How is the description of Ishmael's descendants a fulfillment of the prophecies and promises regarding Ishmael (Genesis 16:12; 21:18)?

6. What is the most important lesson you've learned about Abraham's life that applies to your own situation right now?

Spend some time asking God for greater faith—like that demonstrated by Abraham—to follow God into the unknown.

DAY TWO: **Sibling Rivalry**

Genesis 25:19–28

For God to fulfill the promise to Abraham—to make him the father of many nations through his son, Isaac—Rebekah needs to have a child. But, like Sarah, Rebekah is barren.

1. Read Genesis 25:19–28. How does Isaac's response to his wife's barrenness differ from Abraham's response to Sarah's barrenness (Genesis 16:1–4)?

2. How long does Isaac have to wait for God to answer his prayer for a son? (*Hint*: See Genesis 25:20, 26.)

What does such a long period of waiting reveal about Isaac's faith?

What, for you, is the hardest part of waiting for God to answer a prayer?

3. Several months after Rebekah conceives, she is unsettled when she experiences a jostling in her abdomen. In essence, Rebekah asks God, "Why is this happening to me?" Have you ever asked God a question like this in the midst of a struggle? What was the response?

Jacob is described as being a "peaceful man" who lives among the tents (Genesis 25:27 NASB). The Hebrew word here is *tam* and can be translated "civilized." In other words, while Esau enjoys the outdoors, Jacob prefers a more cultured, refined lifestyle.

4. What signs of rivalry emerge between Jacob and Esau in Genesis 25:22–28?

5. What similarities or differences do you recognize between Jacob and Esau's rivalry and any rival relationship in your life right now?

6. What insights does the story of Jacob and Esau provide that might help you to diffuse any rivalries in your life?

Spend time prayerfully considering any rivalries in your own life. Ask God to bring reconciliation and peace to the relationship. Ask God to transform any areas of anger, unforgiveness, or angst into love for the other person.

DAY THREE: The Winning of the Birthright
Genesis 25:29–34

The birthright is particularly valuable to the oldest son because it ensures a double portion of the family's estate. In ancient culture, a father's inheritance was divided evenly among all of the sons, except for the oldest, who received two portions. In a family with only two sons, the older son received everything. This probably became a point of contention for the twins Jacob and Esau, who were born moments apart.

Jacob negotiates a shrewd deal to steal his older brother's birthright. He desires the favored, privileged status of being the firstborn.

For Esau, his future inheritance is on the line. He's famished, and he must make a choice. Rather than refuse Jacob or negotiate the terms of the birthright, Esau reveals his impetuous, rash nature when he agrees to Jacob's outrageous terms. His quick response to Jacob also demonstrates that he doesn't value the birthright. Esau shows no remorse for what he's done. He simply eats, drinks, and goes on his way. Like Judas who denies Jesus for some cash, Esau sets the bar low when he denies his birthright for a hot meal.

1. Read Genesis 25:29 – 34. Use the following chart to list five adjectives each that describe Jacob and Esau.

Jacob	Esau

2. Why do you think Jacob values the birthright more than Esau?

What in your own life do you tend to underappreciate but would greatly miss if it were gone?

3. Of the members of your family, whom do you struggle the most to get along with?

What efforts are you making now to strengthen that relationship?

4. Have you been able to accept the blessings and challenges of the family God has placed you in? Why or why not?

Spend some time praying for the members of your immediate and extended family. Ask God to bless, encourage, protect, and provide for your family. Invite him to show you what you can do to bring about reconciliation in any broken relationships.

DAY FOUR: A Family Torn Apart by Deception
Genesis 26–27

It's been said, "Like father like son," but nowhere is this more apparent in Genesis than when Isaac encounters Abimelek.

1. Read Genesis 26. What elements of Isaac's story are similar to Abraham's?

> **Notable**
>
> Adam, Abraham, and Isaac all cite fear as a reason for hiding the truth (Genesis 3:10; 20:11; 26:9).

Isaac knows that Jacob already has the birthright, but he believes he can still pass his blessing on to his favorite son, Esau. Isaac doesn't realize he has a savvy opponent — his wife. The couple is working against one another, maneuvering and manipulating to get the upper hand for what they want rather than what God wants.

2. Read Genesis 27:1–29. Rebekah presents a deplorable plan to trick Isaac into blessing Jacob instead of Esau. After hearing the plan, what is Jacob's primary concern (v. 12)?

What does this reveal about Jacob's character?

The blessing of the oldest son was meant to be a public event, but Isaac chooses to bless his son in private. On this important day, Isaac should be focused on celebrating the blessing, but instead he tries to keep the blessing a secret. Despite the importance of the occasion, Isaac is distracted by his appetite, as noted by repeated references to food, tasting food, and eating.

3. Read Genesis 27:30–46. How do Isaac and Esau respond to the news of the deception (vv. 33–34)?

Do you think Isaac and Esau's responses were appropriate? Why or why not?

Quotable

"Jacob was on his way, a long meandering way, to becoming Israel."[14]

–H. Stephen Shoemaker

The woman who devised the scheme that caused Esau to hate Jacob must now devise a scheme to save Jacob's life. Rebekah sends Jacob to her homeland and promises to call for him when it's safe. Her favorite son won't return for twenty years.

4. In the previous Afterhours personal study, you were asked to make a list of five adjectives that described Jacob and Esau (page 93). How have you seen the descriptors of each man's character play out in Genesis 26–27?

Bonus Activity

Do you know a pastor, teacher, businessperson, coworker, parent, or leader who could use a kind word of hope and love? Send a homemade card or handwritten letter. Give a gift card. Go out of your way to say thanks and encourage them to finish well this week.

---

5. Why do you think Isaac, whose life is marked by miraculous beginnings, reaches such a low point?

What lessons can you learn from Isaac's life on how to finish well?

6. What choices do you need to make now to ensure that you end well in your faith journey?

Spend some time asking God to show you any changes that you need to make in your own life today in order finish well. Ask God for the grace and strength to enact those changes for the long haul.

DAY FIVE: Jacob Encounters God

Genesis 28

Esau is furious at Jacob for stealing both his birthright and blessing. Rebekah worries that if Jacob stays around the house any longer, Esau will kill him. Then,

Esau will be punished and possibly killed as well, leaving her without either of her sons. To protect Jacob, Rebekah advises him to travel to Haran to stay with her brother Laban until Esau cools down. Before Jacob leaves, Isaac pulls him aside to bless him and to offer some specific instruction.

1. Read Genesis 28:1–9. What instructions and blessings does Isaac give Jacob?

   What is significant about the instructions?

   What is significant about the blessings?

Esau realizes that his choice of Canaanite wives displeases his father, so he goes to be with Ishmael near the border of Egypt and marries there. It's interesting to note that Ishmael was the rejected offspring of Abraham, and now the rejected son of Isaac goes to live among his descendants.

> **Notable**
>
> The distance that Jacob traveled from Beersheba to Harran (Genesis 28:10) is approximately 550 miles and probably took Jacob more than a month.

2. Read Genesis 28:10–22. Jacob has an unforgettable dream. In the space below, draw a picture of the image Jacob saw in his dream. Why do you think God used this image to communicate to Jacob?

Has God ever used a dream to communicate to you? If so, how did the dream impact your faith?

3. Why do you think God took a different approach to pursuing Jacob than he used to pursue Abraham or Isaac?

Why do you think God takes different approaches to pursuing different people?

Prior to this encounter with God, Jacob has been recognized as a deceiver and swindler. Yet God still pursues Jacob, knowing he is a work in process.

God approaches Jacob at a vulnerable time. Jacob is a fugitive on the run from his brother, and has traveled hundreds of miles from his family. He probably second-guesses himself daily, wondering if stealing Esau's birthright was really worth it. He may be looking over his shoulder frequently to see if his brother is pursuing him. Jacob certainly doesn't expect to meet God on his journey—so the encounter is unexpected, encouraging, and full of hope and life.

4. Jacob promises to give God a tithe of everything he receives. Why is this significant to the transformation taking place in Jacob's life?

What changes in your own heart and life have you seen when you choose to give financially or otherwise?

Spend some time prayerfully considering if there is anything of your time, talents, or resources that God is calling you to give. Respond to any nudges you sense from God to express God's goodness and love through generosity to others.

It's Not about You

Genesis 28–36

> Incomprehensible and immutable is the love of God. For it was not after we were reconciled to him by the blood of his Son that he began to love us, but he loved us before the foundation of the world, that with his only begotten Son we too might be sons of God before we were any thing at all.
>
> —*St. Augustine of Hippo*

God selected Abraham, a pagan, to become the forefather of the people of God. The Lord chose an infertile woman, Sarah, to give birth to the fulfillment of that divine promise. And now, God makes one of the most startling choices of all: He chooses Jacob to father the twelve tribes of Israel. This is a man who is convinced that it's all about him. Such self-centered thinking stands in opposition to the love God calls us to. Without the love of God infusing our lives, it is impossible to truly love others. God's love is the fuel for our love, and we burn brighter when we're filled up with the reality of that love.

Getting Started: Select One

Experiential Activity: Balderdash

What you'll need:

♦ The game of Balderdash

1. Spend 15–20 minutes playing a few rounds of Balderdash—a game in which you have to figure out who is telling the truth and choose whom to believe.
2. Discuss the following questions:
   - What do you think it was like to be Jacob's friend or family member knowing he was a master deceiver?
   - Do you find it relatively easy or difficult to deceive someone?
   - What kinds of people are the easiest for you to deceive? The hardest?
   - What situations are most likely to tempt you to deceive someone?
   - What is the outcome of a relationship that is founded or tainted by deception?

Icebreaker Question

If you're not doing the experiential activity, choose one *of the following questions to begin your discussion.*

   - Have you ever been new to an area or felt like an outsider and had someone reach out to you? Describe the experience. What did you learn through it?
   - Describe a situation in the past three months in which you needed to be reminded, "It's not about you!"
   - Make a list of things within our culture that contribute to the "it's all about me" mindset. How do you combat these things in your life?

(20 MINUTES)

As you watch the DVD, use the following outline to take notes on anything that stands out to you.

I felt like I was breathing in Jesus.

In ancient culture the blessing of the eldest son is an event people wanted to attend, but Isaac keeps it a secret. He plans to bless Esau where no one will hear or see.

On the run from Esau, the last thing Jacob expected to encounter was God.

As bad as we may want someone to believe, whether it's a family member, friend, or someone else, ultimately, we are dependent on God working to bring people into a relationship with himself.

Israel, as a man, and a nation, emerges through the wrestling and wounding of God.

I sensed the conviction, the invitation of God's Spirit to change my attitude and behavior.

Group Discussion Questions

1. Consider what you learned about God's love from the Afterhours personal studies or on the DVD. What caught your attention or stood out most to you?

2. Take turns reading Genesis 25:26–34 and 27:6–13. Where do you think Jacob got the idea that it was all about him?

   Briefly describe how thinking "it's all about me" sometimes slips into the following areas of your life:

   Work . . .

   Relationships . . .

   Daily life . . .

3. What disciplines, spiritual practices, or habits have you developed to help you think about others first?

The Birthright and the Blessing

4. Margaret observes, "Jacob, who believes that it's all about him, swindles his brother out of his birthright in exchange for soup and bread. But for Jacob, the birthright isn't enough." In what ways does self-centeredness promote greed?

What other sins do you become prone to when you embrace self-centered thinking and living?

God's Timeline

5. In Genesis 28, God reveals himself to Jacob, who then begins to undergo a transformation. Why do you think God didn't reveal himself to Jacob earlier — *before* Jacob swindled his brother and destroyed his family?

Who in your life do you wish God would reveal himself to faster? Explain.

6. What do you think God is trying to communicate to Jacob by revealing himself as "the God of your father Abraham and the God of Isaac" (Genesis 28:13)?

7. How does God's promise to Jacob in Genesis 28:14 compare to God's promise to Abraham in Genesis 22:17? What does the commitment — to stay with a man who has been a deceptive swindler — reveal about God's love and faithfulness?

Notable

In ancient times, olive oil was poured on objects to dedicate them to God. The process of pouring the oil is known as "anointing."

Jacob experiences the fear of the Lord. He responds in awe and wonder at what has just happened. In order to commemorate the moment, Jacob sets up a pillar and pours oil over it to consecrate it. He names the place Bethel, meaning "house of God." Then Jacob makes a vow to God, a vow which reveals a reorientation in Jacob's life. Jacob makes the commitment to God on the condition that the Lord's presence, protection, and provision remain with him.

Encountering God

8. In Genesis 27:20, Jacob describes God as "your God," but in Genesis 28:20–22 Jacob refers to God as "my God." Why is it important for Jacob's faith to become his own?

When would you say your faith became your own? What circumstances or relationships helped to make it possible?

Encounters with God are unexpected and often transform us. Sometimes they expose our weakness and leave us limping. Yet they invite us into a deeper relationship with God.

9. When in the last three months have you had an encounter with God? How did the experience affect your perspective of God, yourself, or life?

10. Briefly describe a difficulty you are facing in *one* of the following areas:

Your life overall . . .

Your workplace or daily life . . .

Your relationships (family or friends) . . .

Your spiritual life . . .

How might God be using this situation, as he did with Jacob, to cause you to grow, to recognize it's not about you, and to experience God's transforming power?

The story of Jacob is a powerful reminder that no one is beyond the reach of God's transforming power. Though our culture cries, "It's all about you," the Spirit steadily reminds us that it's all about God. When we reorient ourselves, our lives, our everything in a Godward direction, we can't help but experience spiritual transformation.

Close in Prayer

Ask God to:

- Shift your thinking from self-focused to others-focused.
- Provide opportunities for you to serve and give.
- Help you become a more vibrant conduit of God's love and blessing.

Jumpstart

To get an insider's look at the Pursuing God series, bonus features, and freebies, as well as join the online discussion, visit *www.pursuinggodbiblestudy.com*.

To prepare for the next group session, read Genesis 36–50 and tackle the Afterhours personal studies.

Afterhours Personal Studies

Dive deeper into the book of Genesis by engaging in these five personal studies. If you only have time for one, choose Day Five, which will prepare you specifically for the next session.

DAY ONE: Jacob Falls Head Over Heels in Love

Genesis 29:1–30

While traveling toward Harran, Jacob stops for the night and uses a stone for a pillow (Genesis 28:11). That evening he has an unforgettable dream and encounter with God that changes the course of his life. Now Jacob is about to encounter another stone, a much larger one, which will again change his destiny.

1. Read Genesis 29:1–30. What do you think compels Jacob to remove the stone from the well?

   What does Jacob's action reveal about his character and who he has become?

Notable

Stones were placed on top of wells to prevent evaporation, for sanitary reasons — to keep them clean and protect them from wild animals — as well as to prevent people from accidentally falling in.

2. What is Jacob's response to Rachel (Genesis 29:11)?

   Why do you think Jacob weeps?

3. What attracts Laban's attention to Abraham's servant in Genesis 24:30?

   What attracts Laban's attention to Jacob in Genesis 29:13?

   What does this foreshadow about Laban's character?

Laban expects Jacob to work for him for free because he is a family member, but Jacob negotiates with him. Jacob agrees to work for seven years, reducing his status from family member to hired helper in exchange for marrying Laban's younger daughter, Rachel.

> **Notable**
>
> Leah's name means "cow" while Rachel's name means "ewe." Both names are appropriate for a family living in an agrarian world caring for sheep. Yet Laban treats his daughters like barnyard animals that are bartered and sold.

4. Laban pretends to be outraged that Jacob wants to take the younger daughter before the older. How does Jacob reap what he sows in his relationship with Laban?

5. Read Galatians 6:7–8. When have you seen the principle of reaping and sowing revealed in your own life?

Spend some time asking God for wisdom on where you can sow better seed in your life and the lives of others. Ask God to help you to recognize the principle of sowing and reaping in your own life.

DAY TWO: **The Battle of the Brides**

Genesis 29:31–30:43

Leah is described as not being loved. The Hebrew word used here actually means "to be hated." She's rejected and despised but, because of Jacob's agreement with Laban, he cannot divorce her. One can only imagine the loneliness and heartache Leah feels. Yet God sees her pain and loss.

1. Read Genesis 29:31–35. In the following chart, match each of the four sons born to Leah in this passage to the meaning of their names.

Name	Hebrew meaning
Reuben	The LORD has heard
Simeon	I will praise the LORD
Levi	See, a son! The LORD has seen my misery
Judah	My husband will be attached to me

The names of Leah's sons reveal much about her own journey. Leah is in awe that God opens her womb and gives her a child. She knows God has seen her anguish and misery. Then Leah recognizes God's providence and provision in the birth of her second son, though she is still unloved. With the third son Leah is hopeful that she will win over the heart of Jacob. With the birth of her fourth son, Judah, Leah comes to terms with her lot in life and offers praise to God.

Each of Leah's four sons must arouse jealousy in Rachel. As much as Rachel
wants to have a child, she is barren. The two sisters enter into a fierce competition to see who can have the most children.

2. Read Genesis 30:1–24. In what ways do Rachel and Leah each want
    what the other sister has been given?

Do you tend to focus more on what you have or what you don't have?

What is the result?

Rachel doesn't seem to appreciate the fact that she is loved by Jacob, and Leah
doesn't seem to appreciate the fact that she has children. The sisters both reach
a point where they're more focused on what they don't have than what they've
been given.

In their struggle to win Jacob's love—and the social status that comes with
bearing children—Rachel and Leah turn to their maids. At one point, the two
women actually negotiate who will spend an evening with Jacob by bargaining
with a plant called a mandrake. Leah's son Reuben discovers some mandrakes
in a field and brings them to Leah. When Rachel catches sight of the man-

drakes, she wants what her sister has. She offers Jacob to Leah for the evening in exchange for the love fruits. That evening, Leah conceives Issachar, whose name means, "God has rewarded me."

Despite Jacob's prayerlessness, Rachel's bitterness, and Leah's rivalry, God still blesses the family with a dozen sons and a daughter named Dinah, reminding us that God's grace and goodness extend beyond our selfishness and sin.

3. Use the following charts — one for each of Jacob's wives — to identify key information about the twelve sons and one daughter of Jacob, including their birth order and the meaning of their names. Some answers are provided, so use the clues on the chart to fill in *all* the remaining blanks.

Scripture	Leah's children	Meaning of name	Birth order
Genesis 29:32		See, a son!	
	Simeon		
Genesis 29:34			
			4
Genesis 30:17–18			
		Honor	
Genesis 30:21		*Meaning not given*	11

Scripture	Zilpah's sons (Leah's maid)	Meaning of name	Birth order
	Gad		
Genesis 30:12–13		Happy	

Scripture	Rachel's sons	Meaning of name	Birth order
Genesis 30:22–24			12
Genesis 35:16–18			13

Scripture	Bilhah's sons (Rachel's maid)	Meaning of name	Birth order
	Dan		
Genesis 30:7 – 8		My struggle	

4. Rachel and her maid have four children while Leah and her maid have nine. What comfort do you find in knowing that God champions the needs of the weak and unloved?

5. Read Genesis 30:25 – 43. Who do you think acted more shrewdly — Laban or Jacob? Why?

6. Does it surprise you that God uses such a dysfunctional family to give birth to the twelve tribes of Israel? Why or why not?

What hope does this story provide for you that God can use anything and anyone?

Spend some time thanking God for the ways God can redeem even the most broken and messed-up situations. Thank God for the ways your own areas of pain, brokenness, and dysfunction have been healed and redeemed as testimonies of God's goodness and faithfulness.

Jacob and Laban's relationship deteriorates to the point of outright hostilities. God directs Jacob to return to Canaan. Upon hearing the news, Rachel and Leah choose to give up their own family in favor of staying with Jacob, which is a stinging blow to Laban. The shrewd father-in-law chases Jacob down and accuses him of stealing an idol.

1. Read Genesis 31:1–42. In what ways has God used the twenty years of hardship serving under Laban to transform Jacob?

   How have times of hardship transformed you spiritually?

> **Notable**
>
> A portion of the amount of money given for marriage is meant to go to the daughter. In other words, some of the wages Jacob worked fourteen years to earn belong to Rachel and Leah.

2. What do you think compels the women to leave their homeland to go with Jacob?

3. Why do you think Rachel commits the crime of "godnapping" by stealing idols from her father's household?

   Why is it so important that the idols not be found?

4. Read Genesis 31:43–55. In what ways is this scene proof that Laban and Jacob can't agree on anything?

How do you navigate a relationship in which you can't seem to agree on anything?

Going home means Jacob will have to face his brother Esau. Just as Jacob encountered God after his fallout with Esau, he now encounters God before the reconciliation with his brother.

5. Read Genesis 32. What steps does Jacob take to prepare for the meeting with his brother?

How do you prepare for a meeting in which you want to mend a relationship?

Jacob's encounter with God reveals that there's something unexpected and ambiguous about a divine encounter. Divine encounters don't happen on our terms, but God's terms. They surprise us. They often happen at our low points. They remind us of our own weakness. They invite us into deeper relationship with God. Just as Jacob's encounter with God didn't equate to ease and comfort, often ours don't either. Divine encounters remind us that God is fully in control and we are not. Although every encounter with God has a uniquely mysterious element to it, the hallmark of every divine encounter is that we walk (or limp) away as different people.

6. Jacob meets God at night. In the morning, he's a different person. Jacob is now Israel. Have you ever had a situation in which you limped away a better person? Describe.

Spend some time prayerfully reflecting on God-encounter moments in the past when you limped away a better person. Thank God for the opportunities and encounters God has used to grow your faith and transform you into who you are today.

DAY FOUR: Esau, Dinah, and Israel

Genesis 33–36

The challenges Jacob faces stretch his faith, expose his heart, and force him to grow. When Esau meets Jacob for the first time after many years, both men have changed in countless ways.

1. Read Genesis 33. Jacob wrestles God at night and is reunited with his brother later that same day. What do you think surprises Israel most about the encounter?

What do you think surprises Esau most about the encounter?

Following Jacob's reconciliation, a powerful scene unfolds with Jacob's only daughter, Dinah. While living in Canaan, Dinah is raped by prince Shechem. Jacob's sons confront the wrongdoing with violence.

2. Why do you think it's significant that Jacob settles in sight of the city in Genesis 33:18? How did this endanger Dinah?

3. Read Genesis 34. What does the story reveal about Jacob's family?

God continues pursuing a relationship with Jacob (Israel). God calls Jacob to Bethel to build an altar. In response, Jacob purges his household of false gods and asks everyone in his household to cleanse themselves and change their clothes as a symbol that they are living a new and purified way of life. After cleansing his home of idols, Jacob and his family make their way to Bethel. Bethel marks a shift in the life of Jacob.

After God reaffirms the promises to Jacob at Bethel, Rachel dies giving birth to Benjamin. This marks both an end and a beginning for Jacob. The focus of Jacob's story shifts from his wives to his sons.

4. Read Genesis 35. How does Reuben, the oldest son, disqualify himself from ruling over the twelve tribes of Israel (v. 22)?

When have you been tempted to do something that would disqualify you from leadership?

How did you handle the situation?

5. Read Genesis 36, which offers the genealogy of Esau in Canaan as well as his separation from Canaan. Why do you think Esau's genealogy begins with him taking wives from the daughters of Canaan?

What does this reveal about Esau?

Why do you think the death of Esau isn't reported?

Is your own spiritual journey more reflective of Esau or Jacob? Explain.

The twelve tribes of Esau and the land of Edom reflect Esau's choices. Like Ishmael, Esau cuts himself off from the line of blessing by marrying Canaanite wives. Like Lot, he leaves the Promised Land for lands that offer greater prosperity. Despite Esau's poor choices, his descendants benefit from God's faithfulness. Edom becomes a great nation — one that prospers and grows. Deuteronomy 23:7 challenges, "Do not abhor an Edomite, for he is your brother." Yet despite its growth, Edom can never compare to Israel. The older brother will always serve the younger.

6. Read Genesis 37. What surprises you about the initial portrait of Joseph?

In what ways is Joseph like Jacob?

Spend some time prayerfully reflecting on the life of Jacob. Ask God to reveal which lessons from Jacob's life apply to your own life right now.

Following the genealogy of Esau, Genesis 37 begins by noting that Jacob lived in the land of Canaan. This stands in stark contrast to Esau who lived in the hill country of Seir (Genesis 36:9). The mention highlights the choice made by Jacob to remain in the Promised Land.

Now we're introduced to the story of Joseph, the youngest son of Jacob and Rachel, until Benjamin is born later. Just as Esau was Isaac's favorite son, Joseph is Jacob's favorite. The favoritism ignites rivalry among the twelve sons of Jacob.

1. Read Genesis 37. Based on this account of Joseph's actions, list six to eight words you would use to describe Joseph.

   Which of the words you listed might also be used to describe yourself as a teenager?

2. Complete the following chart to identify the actions that cause tension between Joseph and his brothers.

Scripture	Actions that cause tension
Genesis 37:2	
Genesis 37:3 – 4	
Genesis 37:5 – 11	

Reflecting on the chart, do you think the brothers' response to Joseph is justified or unjustified (Genesis 37:19 – 20)? Why or why not?

3. How do you typically respond when you are provoked by someone?

4. Recognizing that the rape at Shechem (Genesis 34) occurred only two years earlier when Joseph was fifteen, do you think Jacob is wise to send his Joseph to Shechem (Genesis 37:13)? Why or why not?

What does Jacob's decision reveal about him?

Notable

Twenty shekels of silver was equivalent to approximately five years' wages for a shepherd.

5. Not only do Joseph's brothers want to kill Joseph's dreams; they want to kill the dreamer. Have you ever had your dreams intentionally squashed by someone else? If so, how did you respond?

Have you ever been the one to squash someone else's dreams? If so, how did you feel afterward?

6. How have you responded to the opposition or struggle in your own life as you've sought to fulfill a God-given dream?

Spend some time asking God to reignite any snuffed dreams in your life. Ask God to reveal ways for you to be a source of encouragement for other people's dreams.

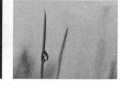

Finding God among Prisons and Palaces

Genesis 37–50

> He who counts the stars and calls them by their names is in no danger of forgetting His own children. He knows your case as thoroughly as if you were the only creature He ever made, or the only saint He ever loved.
>
> *–C.H. Spurgeon*

In the midst of difficult circumstances, we sometimes wonder, "Where is God?" Yet the story of Joseph reveals that no matter what our emotions or circumstances may try to tell us, God is still present and faithful to the promises he has made.

Joseph's story reveals that even though we cannot control circumstances, we can control how we respond to those circumstances. Joseph spent many years in prison and suffered multiple injustices, yet God continued to pursue Joseph and displays a divine plan for the people through Joseph's unexpected rise to power.

Getting Started: Select One

Experiential Activity: From Prison to President

What you'll need:

◆ Information on Nelson Mandela from your local library or online

1. Spend some time researching the life story of Nelson Mandela, a modern leader who spent time both in prisons and palaces.
2. Highlight a few facts about Mandela and consider showing any clips from YouTube or a DVD about Mandela's life.
3. Discuss the parallels between Nelson Mandela and Joseph.

   - What common emotions do you think they felt?
   - What fears do you think they both experienced?
   - What doubts do you think they both shared about their futures?

Icebreaker Question

If you're not doing the experiential activity, choose one of the following questions to begin your discussion.

- Sometimes life doesn't turn out like we expect. What unexpected surprises has life given you?
- What types of situations make you wonder, "Where are you, God?"
- Have you ever had an experience in which someone intended evil or harm but God used it for good? If so, describe.

Six: Finding God among Prisons and Palaces

As you watch the DVD, use the following outline to take notes on anything that stands out to you.

Sometimes life doesn't turn out like you expect.

With jealousy brewing, Joseph should keep a low profile. But it's almost as if he can't help himself.

Life isn't turning out how Joseph expects. On the long caravan ride to Egypt I have a hunch Joseph asked the question, "Where are you, God?"

God uses the most unlikely set of circumstances to preserve and prosper not just Joseph, but his people.

Years before, Joseph's two dreams got him into a dungeon; now, interpreting these two dreams will get him out.

God is present both in the palaces and in the prisons, in the years of feast and the years of famine.

(30 – 45 MINUTES)

1. Consider what you learned about God's love and faithfulness from the After-hours personal studies or on the DVD. What caught your attention or stood out most to you?

The Dreamer

2. Joseph has been given a tremendous gift for dream interpretation, but the way he handles his gift almost gets him killed. How have you seen spiritual gifts misused or abused? What makes the difference?

> **Notable**
>
> Joseph's dreams are the first dreams in the Bible in which God does not speak. The dreams described throughout Joseph's story always come in pairs.

3. Joseph finds great favor with Potiphar, only to be falsely accused and then imprisoned. Joseph rises to favor with the jailer and interprets the dreams of fellow prisoners, only to be forgotten. At some point in life, we all experience some kind of injustice. How do you respond to the times when life isn't fair?

What does the story of Joseph reveal about how to handle these experiences?

Where Is God?

4. Are there any situations in your own life right now where you're wondering, "Where are you, God?" If so, describe.

5. Why do you think the promises of God often require years of waiting and hardship?

How has waiting and hardship shaped your own spiritual growth and character?

When have you experienced God as "I AM"?

6. What do the following passages reveal about what waiting on God through hardship produces in our lives?

Romans 5:3:

1 Peter 2:20–23:

Do you tend to run toward or away from hardship? Explain.

Every Step of the Way

7. In our faith journeys, we encounter times when we need to move forward and take risks and other times when we need to wait patiently and pray. How do you discern when you're supposed to move forward and when you're supposed to wait?

> **Notable**
>
> Joseph's dream in Genesis 37:7 of his brothers (represented by the sheaves) bowing down is fulfilled in progressive stages. His brothers bow once in Genesis 42:6, twice in Genesis 43:26, 28, and then throw themselves at his feet in Genesis 50:18.

8. When Joseph encounters his brothers, he tests them multiple times before revealing himself to them. Why do you think Joseph tests them?

   Have you ever tested anyone to see if they've changed or been transformed? If so, describe.

9. The original temptation of Adam and Eve in the garden circled around the question of whether or not God really loves us. In other words, is God good and loving and can God be trusted? In what ways have you discovered that God is loving and good and faithful as you've studied the book of Genesis?

Mary Benson – health
Craig Denney – lymphoma
Tiara – leukimia 6yrs

> **Notable**
>
> Joseph lives both the first and the last seventeen years of his life with Jacob (Genesis 37:2; 47:28), signifying the perfect timing of God in his life.

10. Reflecting on your study of *Pursuing God's Love*, how would you describe what it means to serve the God of Abraham, Isaac, and Jacob?

Why is it important to pursue God's love in your own life?

The story of Joseph is a powerful reminder that even when things don't make sense, God is still at work. When we wonder, "Where are you, God?" we can trust that God is more involved than we can ever imagine.

 ## Close in Prayer

Ask God to:

- Continue revealing God's presence and guidance in your life.
- Provide opportunities to use the unique gifts you've been given.
- Give you courage to walk faithfully into all God has for you.

 ## Jumpstart

To get an insider's look at the Pursuing God series, bonus features, and freebies, as well as join the online discussion, visit *www.pursuinggodbiblestudy.com*.

Tackle the Afterhours personal studies and consider organizing a final gathering to connect, share a meal, and hang out with your group. If you enjoyed this study, consider another six-week DVD study in this series called *Pursuing God's Beauty: Stories from the Gospel of John*, which invites you to dig deeper into God's Word by exploring this magnificent book of the Bible.

> ### Bonus Activity
>
> If Andrew Lloyd Webber's *Joseph and the Amazing Technicolor Dreamcoat* is playing in your area, consider gathering a group of friends to attend the performance. Or consider watching it on DVD. Reflect on how the play follows the biblical story and where the story heads in a different direction.

Afterhours Personal Studies

Dive deeper into the book of Genesis by engaging in these five personal studies.

DAY ONE: Unlikely Faith

Genesis 38

If the rivalry among Jacob's sons with Joseph wasn't enough, we're now given a glimpse into another of Jacob's sons, Judah. He leaves his family in order to take up residence among the Canaanites and ends up marrying a Canaanite woman. Together they have had three sons: Er, Onan, and Shelah. Judah selects a woman named Tamar to marry his oldest son, Er. The Scripture notes that because Er was evil, God took his life. This is the first time in Scripture that explicitly says God put someone to death.

Er's death leaves Tamar in a predicament. According to the law of the time, the brother of the deceased is responsible to marry the widow and raise up a son in the brother's name. Thus, Judah's second son, Onan, is required to marry Tamar and have children. Although he proceeds to marry Tamar, Onan knows any children won't be his and so he ensures she doesn't become pregnant. God takes Onan's life, too.

> **Notable**
>
> The name Er in Hebrew is known to spell "evil" backward.

Both of Tamar's husbands have died. The last thing Judah wants is for his third son to experience a similar fate. Instead of marrying her to Shelah, he sends the widow away to live with her father. Rather than marry a Canaanite husband, she remains true to Judah's family in a daring act of faith and becomes the heroine of the story.

1. Read Genesis 38. While Genesis 37 offers a detailed look at the character of Joseph, Genesis 38 provides a detailed look at the character of Judah. What similarities and differences do you note between the two?

2. In ancient culture, women fulfilled one of two major roles. Either they married and produced children for their husband, or they were unmarried and remained virgins in their father's home. With Er's death, Tamar is left in a precarious situation as a barren widow. Why is Judah's response to Tamar wicked?

Tamar knows Judah had no intention to give her his third son, Shelah, in marriage. She plots to outsmart Judah by matching deception with deception. Tamar may have been familiar with ancient laws that suggest that if a married man and his brothers all died, the father is responsible for her. Judah unwittingly hires Tamar as a prostitute. As a promise of payment for her services, she asks for his signet ring, cord, and staff. In modern terms, this would be like asking for a man's wallet with his identification, credit cards, and social security card tucked inside.

When Judah wakes up the next day he realizes he's made a foolish mistake and asks his friend Hirah to retrieve his possessions and pay the woman.

Notable

Four women are mentioned in the genealogy of Jesus in the Gospel of Matthew. All of the women — Tamar, Rahab, Ruth, and Bathsheba — are outsiders to Israel and their marriages are marked by scandal, yet God notes their faith and deems them worthy.

3. Reflecting on Genesis 38:15 – 24, do you think Judah has more concern for Tamar as the prostitute or as his daughter-in-law?

When Judah discovers what he's done, he takes responsibility for Tamar and acknowledges her righteousness. Judah honors Tamar as a bride. Though Judah's two sons had died, Tamar gives birth to two more sons—Perez and Zerah—who will carry on the family name. The sons' names can be translated "bursting forth" (Perez) and "shining forth" (Zerah). The names reflect Perez's bursting forth to become the firstborn and the favor that reflected on Judah as Zerah and his brother were born.

4. Would you describe Tamar as a victim or an overcomer? Explain.

Reflecting on your own life, would you describe yourself more as a victim or an overcomer?

Quotable

"It may seem a bit strange to put the word 'redeemer' with Tamar, but in the Hebrew scripture the word 'redeemer' means 'to take responsibility for' and refers to persons who take responsibility for others and who call people to responsibility. A redeemer, then, is one who keeps life and love alive, who sees people do right by each other, and who keeps the family going and the community intact."[17]

–H. Stephen Shoemaker

---

5. What signs of transformation appear in Judah's life (Genesis 38:26)?

How is God honored when you take responsibility for your actions?

God promises Perez's offspring will not only be plentiful but royal. Judah is selected as the carrier of royal lineage, despite having evil sons. Because of Tamar's faithfulness, this promise is fulfilled. Ten generations separate King

David from Perez (Ruth 4:18–22). Thus, Perez's emergence ahead of his brother is significant and places him in the line of the Messiah.

Spend some time prayerfully considering if there are any areas of your life in which you've failed to take responsibility. Ask God to give you the courage and strength to walk in integrity and do the right thing.

DAY TWO: Highs and Lows of Joseph's Journey
Genesis 39–41

After being sold into slavery, Joseph finds favor with his master and he's eventually appointed head of the entire household. Then Potiphar's wife makes a sexual advance toward Joseph. When Joseph rejects her, she falsely accuses him of impropriety and he's sent to prison.

1. Read Genesis 39. Why is it significant that the author of Genesis notes that the Lord was with Joseph (Genesis 39:2, 21)?

   What types of situations tend to challenge your belief that God is with you?

2. Judah faces sexual temptation in Genesis 38 and now Joseph faces sexual temptation in Genesis 39. How does each respond and what is the result?

   When are you most likely to experience sexual temptation in your own life?

What helpful habits or practices do you use to resist sexual temptation?

While in prison, Joseph finds favor with the prison warden who shows him kindness or *hesed*, the Hebrew word meaning to act with love and loyalty (Genesis 39:21). Two other servants are thrown in prison: the king's cupbearer and the king's cook. Each has an unusual dream, which Joseph interprets.

> **Quotable**
>
> "The ingratitude of the Egyptian cupbearer prefigures the later national experience of the Israelites in Egypt (Exodus 1:8)."[18]
>
> —Nahum M. Sarna

3. Read Genesis 40. Do you think the cupbearer's forgetfulness of what Joseph has done for him is due to a mental or a moral lapse or something else? Explain.

What does the forgetfulness reveal about the cupbearer?

Is there anyone in your life that you've forgotten who, like the cupbearer, you need to remember and show thanks to?

> **Bonus Activity**
>
> Who has invested extra time in your life? Take time to write notes or make calls to express gratitude.

Two years after the cupbearer's life was spared, the king of Egypt has two dreams that beg interpretation. The cupbearer finally remembers Joseph. Joseph interprets the king's dreams and then is made the governor over Egypt.

4. Read Genesis 41. Joseph's gift of dream interpretation suggests he has access to a higher power and authority than the Pharaoh of Egypt. What does Joseph's gift of dream interpretation reveal about God?

How does Joseph acknowledge God in his dream interpretations (Genesis 41:16, 25, 28)?

Overall, do you find yourself quick or slow to ascribe thanks to God when he works in your life? Place an X on the continuum to indicate your response.

I AM SLOW TO GIVE THANKS.   I AM QUICK TO GIVE THANKS.

5. God doesn't just give Joseph the dream of his brothers bowing down to him once, but twice. Often when God speaks to us, the louder the message, the more difficult the journey. In what ways have you found this to be true in your own life?

Spend some time reflecting on the highs and lows of your own faith journey. Thank God for loving you and pursuing you every step of the way.

DAY THREE: When Dreams Come True

Genesis 42–45

Pharaoh acknowledges that the Spirit of God is with Joseph. The Hebrew word for "Spirit" is *ruah* and can be translated "wind." The same word, *ruah*, is used in the creation story in Genesis 1:2 when it speaks of the Spirit hovering over the waters. After more than a dozen years of unjust treatment, Joseph is placed in the second position of power in all of Egypt. When the seven years of plenty that Joseph predicted come to an end, famine strikes the land. Jacob and his sons are afflicted. Ten of Joseph's brothers travel to Egypt to buy grain.

1. Read Genesis 42. Why do you think Joseph chooses not to reveal himself to his brothers?

2. What signs of transformation do you see in Jacob's sons in Genesis 42?

3. Read Genesis 43. The servant tells the brothers *shalom*, meaning "peace," or what we might describe as "it's all right" when they describe the silver found in the grain sacks. In what ways is *shalom* or peace restored among the brothers in Genesis 43?

4. Read Genesis 44–45. Why is the brothers' response, in particular that of Judah (Genesis 44), so important for the family reconciliation that takes place in Genesis 45?

5. Joseph reveals his identity to his brothers. He reassures them that he harbors no desire for revenge and that God has used what they meant for harm to accomplish good. What do the following passages reveal about the idea that God is working to bring about what is good?

   Proverbs 16:1–4:

   Proverbs 20:24:

   Proverbs 27:1:

6. At first glance, portions of Joseph's story seem to be attributed to "happenstance" but turn out to be "divine circumstance." Do you tend to attribute the events in your life more to happenstance or to divine circumstance?

How does your perspective affect your personal journey with God?

Spend some time reflecting on the challenges you're facing in life right now. Ask God to give you a divine perspective on situations and circumstances that God wants to use to glorify himself.

DAY FOUR: The End of the Beginning

Genesis 46–50

The reuniting of Jacob and Joseph is a powerful moment of family reconciliation and joy. After his family's arrival, Joseph carefully negotiates the land of Goshen for his family.

Goshen is the best of the land, ideal for grazing animals. Since shepherding is a profession despised by Egyptians, relocating to Goshen also protects Joseph's family by keeping them separate from the Egyptians. The request also signifies to Pharaoh that the Israelites don't have a political agenda and aren't a threat. On this land the Israelites prosper and multiply.

1. Read Genesis 46–48. Why do you think God reassures Jacob of his promises?

When in your spiritual journey do you most need to be reminded of God's promises?

2. Under Joseph's leadership, the Egyptians become slaves. According to the following passages, what do the people give and receive in exchange?

    Genesis 47:14:

    Genesis 47:16:

    Genesis 47:19–20:

    What kinds of things do you tend to become enslaved to without realizing that it's happening?

3. Read Genesis 49–50. Upon their father's death, how do Joseph's brothers try to protect themselves (50:15–18)?

    What is Joseph's response (50:19–21)?

What does this reveal about Joseph's character?

What opportunities has God been giving you recently to refine your character?

4. Though embalmed in Egypt, Jacob is buried in the Promised Land (Genesis 50:4–14). Why is this significant to the promise God gave to Abraham many years before (Genesis 12:1–3)?

What does Jacob's burial in the Promised Land reveal about God's love, pursuit of humankind, and faithfulness?

Spend some time reflecting on the ways God has displayed faithfulness to you over the last decade. Thank God for his presence and persistence in your life.

> **Bonus Activity**
>
> Now that you've read and studied six stories from Genesis, take some time to create a short outline of the book of Genesis. This can be as simple as outlining the general chapters in which major stories are told. After you develop your outline, take time committing the outline to memory. That way when you need to find a story from Genesis quickly in your Bible, you'll have a good idea of where to turn!

DAY FIVE: Reflecting on the Love of God in Genesis

After engaging in a Bible study, sometimes it's easy to move on to the next one without taking time to reflect on what God has been communicating to you. Like a traveler on a long road trip, you can wake up and wonder, "Where have I just been?"

1. Spend a few moments flipping through the pages of your participant's guide. Which statements or notes did you underline or highlight?

   Why were these meaningful to you?

2. What did you learn through this study that you'd never known before about the book of Genesis?

   How do these insights impact your relationship with Jesus?

3. Why is it important to continue pursuing God's love in your own life? What practical steps can you take to do so?

4. Where have you seen God's love most clearly displayed in Genesis?

5. One of the foundational truths of Genesis traces back to the opening words, "In the beginning God." In what ways has your own faith in God been strengthened through this study?

Spend time thanking God for all that you've learned through this study about God's love and presence in our world. Ask God for the grace not only to experience the love of God but also to reflect it in your everyday life.

Notes

1. N. T. Wright, *After You Believe: Why Christian Character Matters* (San Francisco: HarperOne, 2010), 62.

2. H. Stephen Shoemaker, *Godstories: New Narratives from Sacred Text* (Valley Forge, Pa.: Judson Press, 1998), xv.

3. *http://www.smithsonianmag.com/science-nature/Galileos-Vision.html.*

4. John H. Walton, *The NIV Application Commentary: Genesis* (Grand Rapids: Zondervan, 2001), 231.

5. C. S. Lewis, *God in the Dock: Essays on Theology and Ethics* (Grand Rapids: Eerdmans, 1979), 152–153.

6. Nahum M. Sarna, *Understanding Genesis: The Heritage of Biblical Israel* (New York: Schocken Books, 1966), 30.

7. *http://thinkexist.com/quotes/curtis_mcdougall/.*

8. Anne Graham Lotz, *The Magnificent Obsession: Embracing the God-Filled Life* (Grand Rapids: Zondervan, 2009), 21.

9. Celia Brewer Sinclair, *Interpretation Bible Studies: Genesis* (Louisville: Westminster John Knox Press, 1999), 40.

10. Walter Brueggemann, *Genesis: A Bible Commentary for Teaching and Preaching* (Atlanta: John Knox Press, 1982), 140.

11. Claus Westermann, *Genesis 12–36: A Commentary* (Minneapolis: Augsburg, 1985), 311.

12. John Calvin, *A Commentary on Genesis,* ed. and trans. J. King (London: Banner of Truth, 1975), 373.

13. *http://www.pbs.org/wgbh/questionofgod/ownwords/mere2.html.*

14. Shoemaker, 53.

15. Karen Armstrong, *In the Beginning: A New Interpretation of Genesis* (New York: Ballantine, 1996), 86.

16. John C. L. Gibson, *Genesis,* Daily Study Bible vol. 2 (Philadelphia: Westminster Press, 1982), 200–202.

17. Shoemaker, 75.

18. Nahum M. Sarna, *JPS Torah Commentary: Genesis* (Philadelphia: Jewish Publication Society, 1989), 280.

Bibliography

Alexander, T. Desmond and David W. Baker. *Dictionary of the Old Testament Pentateuch.* Downers Grove, Ill.: InterVarsity Press, 2003.

Arthur, Kay. *Teach Me Your Ways: Genesis/Exodus/Leviticus/Numbers/Deuteronomy.* Eugene, Ore.: Harvest House, 1994.

Briscoe, D. Stuart. *The Communicator's Commentary: Genesis.* Waco, Texas: Word, 1987.

Brueggemann, Walter. *Interpretation: Genesis.* Atlanta: John Knox Press, 1982.

Buttrick, George Arthur. *The Interpreter's Bible: General and Old Testament Articles, Genesis and Exodus,* Vol. 1. Nashville: Abingdon, 1980.

Friedman, Richard Elliott. *Commentary on the Torah.* San Francisco: HarperSanFrancisco, 2001.

Hamilton, Victor. *The New International Commentary on the Old Testament: The Book of Genesis, Chapters 1–17.* Grand Rapids: Eerdmans, 1990.

Hummel, Charles and Anne. *Genesis: God's Creative Call.* Downers Grove, Ill.: InterVarsity Press, 2000.

Keck, Leander E., ed. *The New Interpreter's Bible: General and Old Testament Articles, Genesis, Exodus, and Leviticus.* Nashville: Abingdon, 1994.

The Learning Bible (Contemporary English Version). New York: American Bible Society, 2000.

Lucado, Max. *Life Lessons with Max Lucado: Book of Genesis.* Waco, Texas: Word, 1997.

Moyers, Bill. *Genesis: A Living Conversation.* New York: Doubleday, 1996.

Newbigin, Lesslie. *A Walk through the Bible.* Vancouver: Regent College, 1999.

Sarna, Nahum M., ed. *The JPS Torah Commentary: Genesis.* Philadelphia: Jewish Publication Society, 1989.

Shoemaker, H. Stephen. *GodStories: New Narratives from Sacred Texts.* Valley Forge, Pa.: Judson Press, 1998.

Waltke, Bruce K. *Genesis: A Commentary.* Grand Rapids: Zondervan, 2001.

Westermann, Claus. *Genesis 1–11: A Commentary.* Minneapolis: Augsburg, 1974.

Wiesel, Elie. *Messengers of God: Biblical Portraits and Legends,* trans. Marion Wiesel. New York: Random House, 1976.

Williams, Michael E., ed. *The Storyteller's Companion to the Bible: Genesis,* Vol. 1. Nashville: Abingdon, 1991.

About the Author

A popular speaker at churches and leading conferences such as Catalyst and Thrive, Margaret Feinberg was recently named one of the "30 Emerging Voices" who will help lead the church in the next decade by *Charisma* magazine and one of the "40 Under 40" who will shape Christian publishing by *Christian Retailing*. She has written more than two dozen books and Bible studies including the critically-acclaimed *The Organic God*, *The Sacred Echo*, *Scouting the Divine* (Zondervan) and their corresponding DVD Bible studies. She is known for her relational teaching style and for inviting people to discover the relevance of God and the Scriptures in a modern world.

Margaret and her books have been covered by national media including: CNN, the Associated Press, *Los Angeles Times*, *Dallas Morning News*, *Washington Post*, *Chicago Tribune*, *Newsday*, *Houston Chronicle*, Beliefnet.com, Salon.com, USATODAY.com, MSNBC.com, RealClearPolitics.com, Forbes.com, and many others.

Margaret currently lives in Colorado with her 6'8" husband, Leif. When she's not writing or traveling, she enjoys anything outdoors, lots of laughter, and their superpup, Hershey. But she says some of her best moments are spent communicating with her readers. So go ahead, drop her a note:

Margaret Feinberg
P.O. Box 441
Morrison, CO 80465

www.margaretfeinberg.com
info@margaretfeinberg.com

"Like" on Facebook
Follow on Twitter: *@mafeinberg*

margaretfeinberg.com

Great Resources for You and Your Small Group
at www.margaretfeinberg.com

On the site, you'll find:

-Weekly giveaways
-Free e-newsletter sign-up
-Margaret's personal blog
-Interactive discussion board

-Video and audio clips
-Secret sales and promotions
-Travel schedule
-Great prices on Bible studies